VOLUME 9 OF 20 VOLUMES
FRONTIER PRESS COMPANY
COLUMBUS, OHIO

THE LINCOLN LIBRARY OF SPORTS CHAMPIONS

FERGUSON JENKINS, BRUCE JENNER, DON JOHNSON, EARVIN JOHNSON, JACK JOHNSON, RAFER JOHNSON, WALTER JOHNSON, BERT JONES, BOBBY JONES, DEACON JONES, PARNELLI JONES, SAM JONES, JOAN JOYCE, ALBERTO JUANTORENA, SONNY JURGENSEN, DUKE KAHANAMOKU, AL KALINE, ALEX KARRAS, JOHN KELLY, SR. & JACK KELLY, LEROY KELLY, RED KELLY, BILLY KIDD, HARMON KILLEBREW, JEAN-CLAUDE KILLY, BILLY KILMER.

FIRST EDITION
© SPORTS RESOURCES COMPANY 1974
SECOND EDITION
© SPORTS RESOURCES COMPANY 1978
THIRD EDITION
COPYRIGHT © 1981 BY
THE FRONTIER PRESS COMPANY.
ALL RIGHTS RESERVED UNDER
UNIVERSAL COPYRIGHT AND
PAN AMERICAN CONVENTIONS.
PRINTED IN U.S.A. LIBRARY OF CONGRESS
CATALOG CARD NUMBER 80-54174.
ISBN: 0-912168-07-2.
NO PART OF THIS WORK MAY BE REPRODUCED
OR USED IN ANY FORM OR BY ANY MEANS,
ELECTRONIC OR MECHANICAL, INCLUDING
PHOTOCOPYING, RECORDING, OR BY ANY
INFORMATION SYSTEM WITHOUT PERMISSION IN
WRITING FROM THE FRONTIER PRESS COMPANY.

Jenkins, Ferguson

(Fergie) (1943-   ), baseball player, was born in Chatham, Ontario, Canada. A versatile athlete, Jenkins starred in hockey and basketball in high school before choosing a career in professional baseball. Signed by the Philadelphia Phillies in 1962, Fergie spent most of four seasons in the minor leagues. Traded to the Chicago Cubs in 1966, he was used as a relief pitcher that year. Given a chance to be a starting pitcher in 1967, Jenkins reeled off 20 victories. Every season from 1967-1972, he won 20 or more games. His amazing durability allowed him to hurl over 300 innings in four of those six years. Known

for his control, Jenkins won the 1971 Cy Young Award as the National League's (NL) top pitcher. That year, he had a 24-13 won-lost record. He joined the Texas Rangers for 1974 and was named the American League (AL) Comeback Player of the Year after posting 25 wins that season. Jenkins was traded to the Boston Red Sox in 1975 and was dealt back to Texas in 1977.

Some people can walk into a room and create instant excitement. Others can do cartwheels and no one will notice. Ferguson Jenkins is one of those people nobody notices.

Jenkins was baseball's most consistent pitcher during the late 1960's and early 1970's. Yet despite his record, he has never had much public acclaim.

For sheer determination and strength, the 6-foot, 5-inch, 205-pound Jenkins has had few equals. Pitching for the Chicago Cubs, the Canadian-born right-hander won 20 or more games for six straight seasons from 1967 through 1972.

In four of those seasons he hurled over 300 innings.

Jenkins won 25 games with the Texas Rangers in 1974. He became the fourth pitcher in history to win 100 games in both leagues in 1980. Still, he did not gain the fame of a Vida Blue or a Tom Seaver.

Part of the problem lies in Jenkins himself. He is very quiet. During the off-season, while other pitchers make speeches and get their names in the papers, Jenkins goes home to Ontario and spends the winter relaxing.

Nor is Ferguson Jenkins' style of pitching the kind that draws big crowds. He seems more like a businessman on the mound. Instead of blowing fast balls past hitters as Blue and Seaver do, Jenkins depends on near-perfect control—a subtle talent that seldom brings crowds to their feet.

"All I try to do is throw strikes," he says. "I want to make them hit the ball. And I try to help the fielders by pitching quickly. It keeps them alert."

In peak form, Jenkins is out on the mound every four days. In both the National League (NL) and the

American League (AL), he has been among the leaders in games and innings pitched.

He also has another special quality. He gets tougher as the game goes on. Most of the runs scored against him come in the early innings. When a game is on the line in the late innings, he is at his best.

"Fergie's beautiful," said his former manager Leo Durocher. "What I like best about him is that he's not afraid to challenge the hitters. He sees Hank Aaron and says, 'Okay, Hank, here's my fast ball—try to hit it.'"

Yet Ferguson Jenkins does not always win the battle. Every year, he is among the league-leaders in giving up home runs. But it does not seem to bother him. He would rather give up an occasional homer or two than change his pitching pattern.

Not many hurlers can equal Jenkins for day-in-day-out control. He gives up very few walks and has a wide range of pitches he can choose from. He prefers to finesse a batter rather than breeze the ball past him.

Born in Chatham, Ontario, Canada, on December 13, 1943, Ferguson Arthur Jenkins was destined to be an athlete. He was an excellent hockey and basketball player in high school. Because of his height, he considered a career in

The Sporting News *selected Jenkins as the National League Pitcher of the Year in 1971.*

Jenkins, Ferguson

In this sequence, Jenkins shows his powerful wind-up.

Jenkins, Ferguson

basketball, but he turned to baseball to follow in his father's footsteps. Ferguson Jenkins' father was a fine player who once barnstormed through Canada with a black All-Star team.

Jenkins is proud of his black Canadian heritage and the good life he lives in Ontario. "My family has been there for three generations. My father's family was from the Bahamas, my mother's family were slaves, but I don't know where. It's not in the family Bible. But I'll never forget the warmth of the people I grew up with. My roots are still in Canada," says Jenkins.

Jenkins was signed by the Philadelphia Phillies in 1962. He spent most of his first four seasons in the minors before getting his chance in the majors. His big break came in 1966, when the Phillies traded him to the Chicago Cubs. The Cubs used him as a relief pitcher that year. In 61 games, he piled up a 6-8 record with a 3.33 earned-run average (ERA).

Jenkins had earned his chance as a starter. The next year he began his series of six straight 20-victory seasons by posting a 20-13 record with a 2.80 ERA. He also led the league that year by pitching 20

Fergie Jenkins won 20 games for the Chicago Cubs in 1967 and then switched to basketball for a short tour. Joining the famous Harlem Globetrotters, Jenkins played in seven games.

After winning the Cy Young Award in 1971, Jenkins relaxes in the stands at Wrigley Field in Chicago.

With Texas, Jenkins was the 1974 AL Comeback Player of the Year.

complete games.

The following season, he proved that 1967 was not just a fluke. He posted a 20-15 record and a nifty 2.63 ERA. Jenkins worked 308 innings, walking only 65 batters.

In 1969, he had another 20-victory season, posting a record of 21-15 and a league-leading 273 strikeouts. That year, he started 43 games and worked 311 innings. The Cubs battled for the pennant down to the wire before losing the Eastern Division title to the New York Mets.

In 1970, Jenkins led the league with 24 complete games. He worked 313 innings and posted a 22-16 record. Then, in 1971, he reached the pinnacle of his career by winning the league's Cy Young Award. He posted a 24-13 record with a 2.77 ERA.

His 1971 showing finally earned him a little more money, if not public recognition. Ferguson Jenkins, who had been fighting the Cubs' management every year for more money, finally reached the $100,000-a-year salary bracket.

Jenkins again pitched well in 1972. He managed to win 20 games for the sixth straight year, with a 20-12 record and a 3.21 ERA.

After a poor year in 1973, the Cubs traded Jenkins to the Texas Rangers. He responded by pitching a league-leading 29 complete games. He posted a 25-12 record and a 2.83 ERA. Fergie was named the AL Comeback Player of the Year.

Jenkins played the 1975 season with the Rangers and was then dealt to the Boston Red Sox. He won 22 games in two years for the Red Sox. Traded back to Texas, he won 18 games in 1978 and 16 games in 1979, giving him 247 lifetime victories. He also had 2770 strikeouts—ninth on the all-time list. In his quiet way, Ferguson Jenkins had made his mark on baseball.

Jenner, Bruce (1949-),

decathlon champion, was born in Mount Kisco, New York. As a youth, Bruce's favorite sport was water skiing, which was a family pastime. The Jenners moved to Connecticut to pursue the sport, and Bruce became a three-time East Coast champion. In high school, he became a good pole-vaulter and high jumper, as well as a football player. He won a football scholarship to little Graceland College in Lamoni, Iowa. It was there Jenner took up the decathlon. He competed in his first decathlon at the 1970 Drake Relays when he was a sophomore. Jenner made the U.S. Olympic team in 1972 and finished 10th at Munich, West Germany. In 1973, he moved to San Jose, California, for training purposes. He won 12 of 13 meets over

the next three years. Twice he set the decathlon world record for points. At the 1976 Olympics in Montreal, Quebec, Canada, Jenner was brilliant. His 8618 points established a world record and won him a gold medal. Bruce Jenner was named the 1976 Sullivan Award winner as the outstanding amateur athlete in America.

Bruce Jenner had all the makings of an Olympic decathlon champion in 1975 as the 1976 Montreal Games approached. He had been a consistent winner and had broken the world record in his demanding sport. Most experts gave him a very good chance to become the decathlon gold medalist at the 1976 Olympics.

But to accomplish that goal, both Bruce and his wife Chrystie had to make sacrifices. Amateur athletes in the United States have to support themselves through the long years of preparation. Jenner's training schedule allowed him only a few hours a week to try to make some money. So, Chrystie dropped out of school and went to work to support his efforts.

Six to seven hours a day, Jenner trained hard to become the "world's greatest athlete," the title given to every decathlon champion. His single-mindedness became comical at times.

"He's working on his technique constantly," said Chrystie a year before the Olympics. "At the grocery store or at the bank, he's going through the motions of throwing the discus, or he's lifting his leg like he's hurdling. I'm sure people think he's crazy."

The two went through some

Decathlon winner Bruce Jenner acknowledges the cheers of the Olympic crowd in Montreal.

Jenner, Bruce

Jenner competes in the decathlon high-jump competition at the Drake Relays in 1975.

At the 1975 Pan-American Games in Mexico City, Jenner placed first in the decathlon even though he missed on this pole-vault attempt.

hard times, wondering if all their sacrificing would be worth it. If Bruce won, he would be world famous and his future would be secure. But if he lost, he would have nothing to show for all his hard work. Together, they decided it was worth the chance.

When Jenner finally won the decathlon on the Olympic field in Montreal, Quebec, Canada, the first one to greet him was Chrystie.

Bruce Jenner was born October 28, 1949, in Mount Kisco, New York. His family was made up of avid water skiers, so they moved to Sandy Hook, Connecticut, when he was young. Bruce later became a water skiing champ, winning the East Coast title three times.

In the decathlon at the 1976 Drake Relays, Jenner clears the last hurdle en route to winning the 110-meter event.

At the 1976 Olympic trials in Eugene, Oregon, Bruce set a personal best in the javelin.

When he entered Newtown (Connecticut) High School, he turned to other sports. He became good at high jumping, pole-vaulting, and playing football.

Football was his favorite sport and he tried for a college scholarship. The only school that responded was little Graceland College in Lamoni, Iowa. Jenner had never heard of it, but he accepted its offer of a $250-per-year athletic scholarship.

At Graceland, he met Chrystie, a minister's daughter. He also met a man who had trained a number of decathlon competitors, track coach L. D. Weldon. Jenner began working on the event as a sophomore.

In the decathlon, an athlete must compete over a two-day period in 10 events to gain points that are given for certain levels of proficiency. The points are added together for a final score.

Bruce competed in his first decathlon in 1970 at the famous

Jenner, Bruce

He finished a surprising sixth place with 6991 points and set a school record. Jenner found that he liked the demanding event. He also liked the idea that a person could excel in more than one undertaking.

"Our whole society is based upon specialists," he once said. "The decathlon goes against that."

Jenner's progress was amazing. By 1972, he was good enough to make the U.S. Olympic team. At the Summer Games in Munich, West Germany, he finished 10th.

After that, Jenner had one goal—a gold medal in 1976. He turned all of his efforts toward that end, with the help of Chrystie, whom he had married. She took a job as an airline stewardess. Then they moved to San Jose, California, where the weather and competition were better. Bruce also got help from his dog Bertha, who romped along with him on his long and lonely workouts.

Bruce became outstanding, winning meet after meet in the next three years. He was ranked as the world's best in 1974 and 1975. He set a decathlon world record in 1975 with 8524 points, and again in 1976 with 8542 points.

At 6 feet, 2 inches, and 195 pounds, Bruce Jenner was the best athlete in the world. He had won 12 of 13 decathlons in the three years leading up to the 1976 Olympics.

He was not as fast as some decathletes, but he was stronger and could jump better. His endurance in the 1500-meter run (just short of a mile) was also amazing.

Jenner was confident. Just before the Olympics at Montreal, Quebec, Canada, he told a *Sports Illustrated* magazine reporter of his goals for the Games in the individual events. They were high —in some events higher than he had ever done.

On the first day of the decathlon competition, Jenner surprised even himself. He began by matching his best time ever, 10.94 seconds, in the 100-meter dash. In the remaining four events that day, Bruce bettered his previous personal highs in each. He long-jumped 23 feet, 8¼ inches; put the shot 50 feet, 4¼ inches; high-jumped 6 feet, 8 inches; and ran the 400 meters in 47.51 seconds.

"Five bests in a row," Jenner exclaimed at the end of the day. "I was shocked."

He was in third place overall— better than he thought he would be. That gave Jenner great con-

Jenner puts the shot at the 1976 Olympic trials in Eugene, Oregon.

Jenner legs out the last event in the 1976 Olympic decathlon competition—the 1500-meter run. He won the race with a time of 4 minutes, 12.61 seconds, and captured the gold medal.

fidence for the next day's competition, which contained his best events.

Bruce began with a time of 14.84 seconds in the 110-meter hurdles. He won his first event by throwing the discus 164 feet, 2 inches. With a pole vault of 15 feet, 9 inches—equaling his best—Jenner took the lead in points. He followed that with a good throw of 224 feet, 9½ inches in the javelin.

Only one event remained—the grueling 1500 meters. Although medal by then, Bruce gave it everything he had.

"The harder I ran, the better I felt," he later said. He was clocked at 4 minutes, 12.6 seconds, the best he had ever done. It gave him a world record 8618 total points and the Olympic gold medal.

"Before the 1500," he said, "I knew that when I crossed the finish line, it would be the last race of my career, so I wanted the pictures in the paper to look good. That picture showed pure emotion, ecstasy. I couldn't have gone out

On his victory lap, Jenner spotted Chrystie struggling with the security guards. He approached her, lifted her onto the field, and whispered, "It's over now."

After the Olympics, Jenner was acclaimed for his greatness. The Amateur Athletic Union (AAU) of the U.S. named him the Sullivan Award winner as America's best amateur athlete in 1976.

There were those who said that Jenner was out only for the money he would make after winning the gold medal. Many thought he was using the decathlon to set up his career in the movies and television. Although he did sign a contract with the American Broadcasting Company (ABC), Jenner disagreed. "That gold medal meant more to me than all the money in the world."

After winning the 1976 Olympic decathlon, Bruce Jenner gets a hug from his biggest supporter—his wife Chrystie.

⬤ Johnson, Don (1940-),

bowler, was born in Kokomo, Indiana. Having little natural ability, Johnson practiced long and hard in the years before joining the Professional Bowlers Association (PBA) tour in 1962. He captured his first tournament title in 1964 and won two tournaments and a berth on the All-America team in 1968. Johnson became nationally recognized in 1970 when he won the Firestone Tournament of Champions. He was just one pin short of rolling a perfect 300 game. Though he is not a stylish bowler and his release is rather jerky, Johnson is one of the

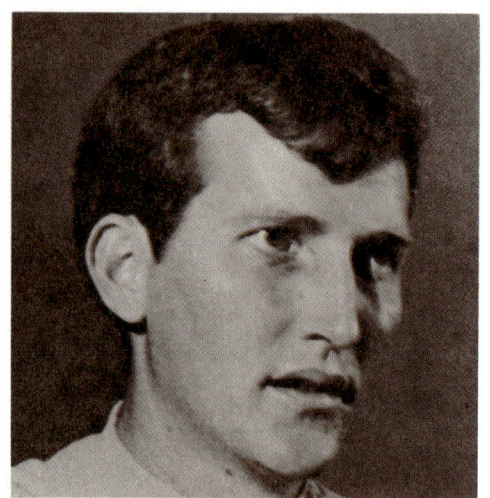

most feared men in one-on-one bowling competition. He was named the Bowler of the Year in 1971 and 1972, winning six and three PBA titles in those respective years. In 1977, he won the 26th PBA tournament of his career—placing him second on the all-time list. Don Johnson was enshrined in the PBA Hall of Fame in 1977.

Don Johnson is a great bowler, and he is certainly a superb psychologist. The "psych-out" technique is a familiar weapon on the sports front, and Don Johnson is a master of its use in bowling. The technique involves giving your opponent a mental needle, a verbal jab, an offhand remark—all intended to unsettle his poise and confidence.

Here is the way Johnson, master psychologist and bowler, talks and behaves at the start of a match. "Man, this pair of lanes is rough! I just don't know how to play 'em. If I go outside, the ball hooks too much. If I play the middle, the ball won't come back into the pocket. I just don't know, just don't know," he laments.

All this talk is accompanied by wringing hands, shaking head, and frowning forehead—all calculated to signal to the mind of his opponent that doom lies just ahead for poor Johnson.

After Don has so slyly set the stage, his antagonist begins to wonder and fuss to himself, "How *do* I play these lanes?" By the time play begins, he is completely confused and uncertain.

Meanwhile, Johnson is making one strike after another. And, yes, the shaking head and wringing hands are still in evidence. The enemy, now thoroughly mixed up, is rolling his bowling balls all over the alley. Before he can "find the line," he is out of the game.

Donald James Johnson was born in Kokomo, Indiana, on May 19, 1940, and speaks with the Midwestern twang of that area. While working on his father's farm, he developed strong arms and shoulders. Country living also gave him time to perfect the bowling technique

Johnson lies on the approach after the ten pin failed to fall. That one pin cost him $10,000 in the 1970 Firestone Tournament of Champions.

16

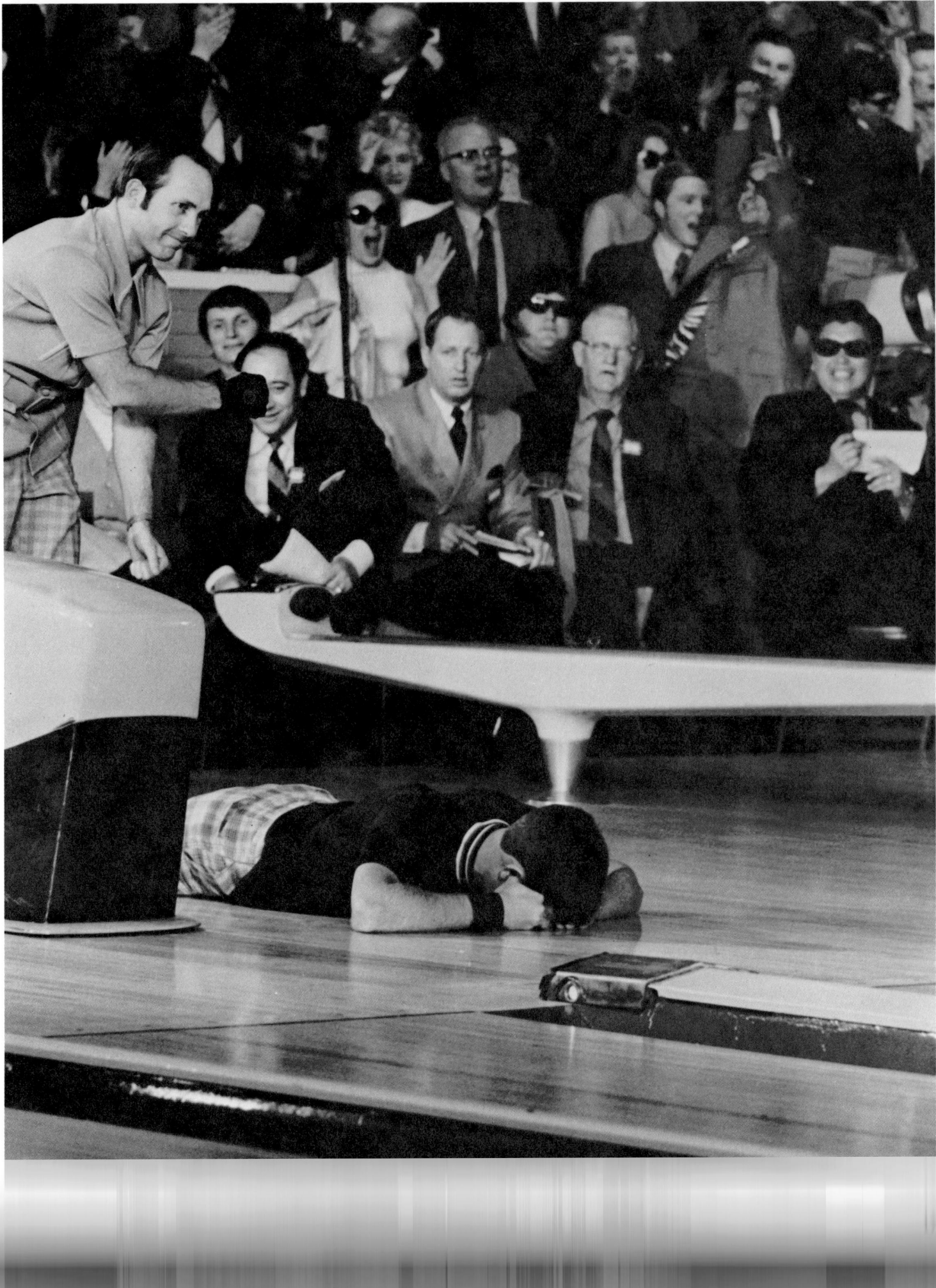

Johnson, Don

Don Johnson and his wife Mary Ann are happy about the trophy he won as the grand prize in the PBA U.S. Open. The smiles may also be about the $10,000 Johnson won in the 1972 event.

that carried him to the top of the Professional Bowlers Association (PBA) in the early 1970's.

The "Kokomo Kid" reached the pinnacle in 1971, when he earned $81,349 while winning six PBA championships. His feats were recognized when he was named Bowler of the Year by his fellow pros and the Bowling Writers Association of America.

The following year he repeated as Bowler of the Year—something only one other bowler (Don Carter) had done in the history of bowling. This time around, the Hoosier won $56,648 on the PBA tour. He started by taking the Bowling Proprietors Association of America U.S. Open. He won again at Denver and captured his third title in Chicago. He just squeezed past Nelson Burton, Jr., in the final balloting, for Burton also had three major wins—at Miami, Milwaukee, and Waukegan.

Johnson's first year on the PBA tour was not sensational. He won a mere $900 as a rookie in 1962. The Midwesterner captured his first tournament title in 1964 at Denver. After that, although a better-than-average performer, he did not draw the spotlight until 1968. Then he took two tournaments, earned $38,990, and was picked for the All-America team. Since then, his selection to the dream team has become almost

Don Johnson has been one of the most successful bowlers on the PBA tour. He was selected Bowler of the Year in 1971 and 1972.

automatic each year.

In the final game of the 1970 Firestone Tournament of Champions, Don Johnson became a household name across the nation. Bowling before a national television audience that numbered in the millions, Johnson strung strike after strike... eight, nine, ten, eleven. He took his stance on the approach for his final pitch, and a ghostly silence settled over Riviera Lanes in Akron, Ohio. He threw a "perfect" ball that settled neatly in the one-three pocket. Cheers thundered out across the nation. Ah, but wait a minute... the ten pin was still standing. In fact, it did not even wiggle.

That one pin cost Johnson $10,000! Who could ever forget that frustrated figure staring in disbelief at that ten pin. Of course, Don's dismay was soothed by the $25,000 first-place check.

"Frustrated? You can say that again," the 5-foot, 10-inch, 150-pounder recalled after the happening. "In all of my bowling days, I never threw a more perfect ball that didn't do it. Sure, winning the Tournament of Champions is a thrill that I'll never forget. Yet, what a kick it would have been to also have hit the 300 game."

Despite his success on the lanes and the adulation that goes to candid personality he was as a newcomer fresh off a Kokomo farm. He frankly admits he is no model as a stylist. He even will confess he has a minimum of natural talent.

"There are many pros on the tour who have a smoother delivery," he says. "Fellows like Dick Weber, Jim Stefanich, and Dave Soutar, just to name three. All are perfection at the point of release. I'm a little jerky and my approach varies.

"I compensate for this by practicing a lot. When I feel myself going into a slump, which isn't difficult to the weakness and work on it. After a bad out, sometimes I'll throw 40 or 50 games before the next tournament starts."

What Don does not mention is a determination as obvious as a watermelon at a peach festival. His fellow pros say they would rather meet almost anyone else on the tour in head-to-head competition. This is surely a testimonial for the slim fellow from Kokomo who now lives in Las Vegas, Nevada.

Early in 1977, Don captured the Midas Open in New Orleans, Louisiana. It was his 26th career victory on the PBA circuit, ranking him second to Earl Anthony among the all-time tournament winners.

Through 1979, Johnson had rolled 22 perfect 300 games. He holds the PBA record for most consecutive years (11) with at least one 300 game.

Johnson claims that his talents are far from unique, and that no bowler ever worked harder to win. "I always have known my physical limitations," he said. "I don't think I will admit to any limitations when it comes to working with what you have and getting the most out of it."

Don Johnson continues to develop as a master strategist, hard worker, and super bowler. In the world of bowling, he should con-

⊛ Johnson, Earvin

(1959-), basketball player, was born in Lansing, Michigan. As a teenager, he received the nickname "Magic" for his sensational ball-handling skills. After leading his high school team to the state championship, he enrolled at Michigan State University. The 6-foot, 8-inch guard helped guide the Spartans to the 1979 National Collegiate Athletic Association (NCAA) title. He was named the Most Valuable Player (MVP) of the NCAA tournament. He also earned All-America honors. Following his sophomore year, Johnson decided to turn professional. The Los Angeles Lakers made him the first choice of the 1979 National Basketball Association (NBA) draft. In 1980, he became the first rookie to start in the NBA All-Star Game since 1969. In the final game of the 1980 championship series, Johnson, starting at center, scored 42 points and grabbed 15 rebounds. Clinching the NBA title for the Lakers, Magic was named the MVP of the playoffs.

After his junior year in high school, Earvin Johnson talked to a reporter from the *Detroit Free Press*. He mentioned a dream he had just had, in which he had gone straight from high school to professional basketball after signing a million-dollar contract for three years. Earvin added that before he woke up from the dream, he had been named the National Basketball Association (NBA) Rookie of the Year.

Earvin "Magic" Johnson's accomplishments in the game of basketball would surpass even his wildest dreams.

A year after his dream, Earvin led his high school team to the 1977 state championship. In 1979, he guided Michigan State University to the National Collegiate Athletic Association (NCAA) title. Johnson was named the Most Valuable Player (MVP) in that tournament. After his sophomore year in college, he joined the Los Angeles Lakers of the NBA. He signed a contract for more than $1 million. As a rookie, Johnson helped lead the Lakers to a world championship and was named the MVP of the NBA playoffs.

In just four seasons, Earvin "Magic" Johnson had played on three championship teams at three different levels of competition. No other player in basketball history had ever accomplished so much in such a short time.

Earvin Johnson, Jr., was born August 14, 1959, in Lansing, Michigan. Earvin, Sr., who held two jobs to support his large family, taught his son to work hard. As a youngster, Earvin learned the game of basketball on the playgrounds. To improve his skills, he played every position.

In 1974, Earvin joined the varsity team at Everett High School. He sparked the squad to a 22-2 record as a sophomore and averaged 24 points a game. Under the guidance of coach George Fox, Johnson improved greatly at the guard position. He continually worked on his

Swarming Celtics apply pressure, but Magic only has eyes for the basket.

passing and dribbling skills. His incredible ball-handling earned him the nickname "Magic" from a sportswriter.

As a senior, Johnson averaged over 40 points for the first few games. Then coach Fox took him aside and suggested that if he shot less, the team's play would improve. Earvin took his coach's advice. His scoring average dropped to 24 points, and Everett won the state title. During the season, Magic's passing, dribbling, and rebounding amazed college and professional scouts.

Johnson attended Michigan State University in Lansing. As a freshman, he led the Spartan basketball team to a 25-5 record. The 6-foot, 8-inch guard averaged just 17 points a game, but he set a school record with 222 assists. He was named to the All-America second team.

Professional scouts began lining up at Earvin's door, but he turned their offers down. He wanted an NCAA championship.

"It was quite a temptation for an 18-year-old kid when Kansas City offered him a million dollars over six or seven years," said Jud Heathcote, the Michigan State coach.

Earvin averaged 17.1 points per game as a sophomore and was named an All-American. More important than points or honors, he led his team to the national title. The Spartans defeated Indiana State University, 75-64, in the championship contest. The brilliant floor leader gave a sparkling display

Johnson, Earvin

Magic looks one way and passes in the opposite direction. As a freshman, he set the Michigan State record for assists.

With the victory net draped around his neck, Johnson waves to the crowd at the 1979 NCAA tournament. Michigan State defeated Indiana State for the title.

After signing with the Los Angeles Lakers, Earvin receives a hug from his mother, Christine.

played Indiana's Larry Bird, the College Player of the Year. Johnson led all scorers with 24 points. He was named the MVP of the tournament.

With a college championship under his belt, Johnson decided to move on to the pro ranks. His charisma and his unselfish, all-round play impressed everyone. The Los Angeles Lakers made Johnson the first choice of the 1979 pro draft. They signed him to a multi-year contract that guaranteed him more than $400,000 each season.

The 20-year-old rookie was determined to live up to his lofty reputation. In his first pro game, he scored 26 points. During a three-game stretch early in the season, he totaled 89 points, 35 rebounds, and 34 assists. Earvin began to draw huge crowds around the league. He also began to instill enthusiasm into his teammates—especially Kareem Abdul-Jabbar.

Opposing players marveled at Johnson's talent and his ability to inspire his teammates. Washington's Elvin Hayes remarked, "The way he brings out the best in a team reminds me of Dave DeBusschere, Bill Russell, Bob Cousy, and Walt Frazier."

Johnson became the first rookie to start in the NBA All-Star Game since Elvin Hayes in 1969. The exciting playmaker went on to lead the Lakers to the Pacific Division title.

During the 1979-1980 regular season, Magic played guard and forward. He averaged 18 points, 7.3 assists, 2.4 steals, and 7.7 rebounds a game. In one five-game stretch, he pulled down an average of 14.8 caroms per contest.

Johnson made his greatest im-

Magic slips past the Portland defense and lays in two points.

pact in the playoffs. He scored, rebounded, and passed well. But, as had always been the case, Abdul-Jabbar emerged as the dominant figure in the early rounds of the playoffs. The Lakers worked their way into the final series with the Philadelphia 76'ers. In the fifth game, Kareem was injured. He had to be left behind in Los Angeles while the team traveled to Philadelphia for the crucial sixth game.

Although the Lakers led the series, 3-2, few believed that they could win the title without their big man. Almost no one gave them a chance when the team announced that Johnson would start the sixth game at center. During the contest, Earvin also played forward and guard.

Magic seemed to be everywhere on the court. He played all but one of the game's 48 minutes, and his contributions were overwhelming—42 points, 15 rebounds, seven assists, and three blocked shots. He made 14 of 23 field-goal attempts and all 14 of his free throws. The Lakers won the game, 123-107, and captured the NBA championship. Johnson was voted the Most Valuable Player in the playoffs, the youngest man ever to receive the honor.

"Magic was unreal," said Julius Erving of the 76'ers. "His potential is unlimited."

23

🥊 Johnson, Jack (1878-1946),

boxer, was born in Galveston, Texas. He began to box in his youth while riding box cars and working odd jobs around the country. Around the turn of the century, Johnson joined a group of touring boxers. One of them gave Johnson some tips on defensive boxing in a jail cell after the two had an illegal bout in Galveston, Texas. In 1902, Johnson headed for California, where he beat many top fighters. He defeated Tommy Burns, a Canadian, in 14 rounds in Melbourne, Australia, to become the first black heavyweight boxing champion of the world in 1908. The idea of a black champion was intolerable to many

whites, and the search for the "Great White Hope" began. Johnson, always a flashy dresser and controversial figure, defended his title until 1915, when at age 37 he was knocked out by Jess Willard in Havana, Cuba. Johnson was killed in an auto accident in 1946. Boxing's greatest authority, Nat Fleischer, called Jack Johnson the greatest heavyweight of them all.

Jack Johnson was the first black fighter to win the world heavyweight boxing championship. Many people think he was the greatest heavyweight fighter of all time.

Out of the ring, Johnson was a free spirit, often breaking the social rules of his day. He was a flashy dresser, a gambler, and a lover of fast cars and high living.

His great success in boxing, his independence, and his bold self-confidence made many black Americans proud of him, even if they did not approve of all the things he did.

In the ring, Johnson was supreme. He was a master boxer, a combination of great strength, graceful style, and tremendous speed. He was unrivaled at picking off punches, feinting, blocking, and counterpunching.

John Arthur Johnson was born in Galveston, Texas, on March 31, 1878. His father was a janitor and a Baptist minister. Jack was a restless boy. He left school after the fifth grade and worked at a variety of jobs. He loved to box. Sometimes he carried two pairs of boxing gloves with him so he could challenge other boys he happened to meet.

When he was 12, Jack Johnson began to roam around the country, "riding the rods" of freight cars. He worked for a while as an exercise boy at a racetrack near Boston. Later he worked on a fishing boat in Florida, and he did some boxing back home in Galveston.

In Chicago, he was taken on as a sparring partner for "Barbados" Joe Walcott (no relation to "Jersey" Joe Walcott). Johnson was soon matched with a fighter named

Jack Johnson (center of the ring) is declared the winner over Pat Lester. The crowd does not seem too pleased with the decision.

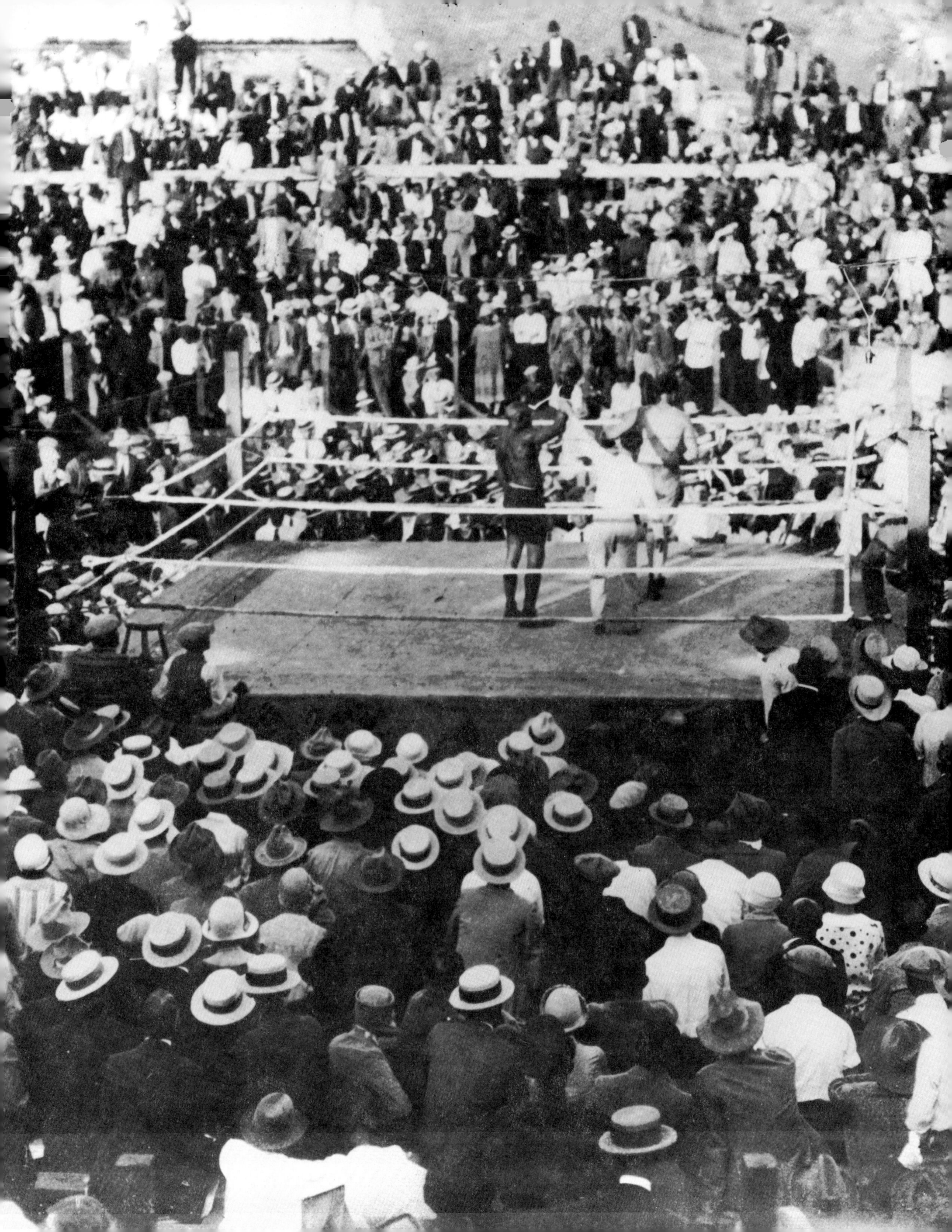

Johnson, Jack

In 1909, Johnson (middle) signs to fight Stanley Ketchel (left). Johnson knocked out Ketchel in the 12th round of their battle.

The champagne flowed in 1909 as Jack Johnson (seated left) signed to fight former heavyweight champion Jim Jeffries.

Klondike, who had a reputation around Chicago. Klondike knocked young Johnson cold.

Johnson joined a group of boxers who were touring and boxing among themselves. Klondike was one of them, and Johnson was able to avenge his Chicago defeat. In Galveston, he fought an illegal bout against Joe Choynski, who knocked him out in three rounds. The police put both of them in jail, where for three weeks Choynski gave Johnson lessons in the art and science of boxing.

In 1902, Johnson boxed in California, where he beat George Gardiner, one-time light-heavyweight champion. Among the top black fighters Johnson defeated were Hank Griffin, Ed Martin, Sam Langford, and Joe Jeannette.

Johnson's star was rising. But early in 1905, Johnson lost to Marvin Hart, the top white contender for the heavyweight title, in a questionable decision. The loss was a blow to Johnson's hopes of getting a shot at the crown.

There had been great black heavyweights before Johnson, among them Tom Molineaux and Peter Jackson. And there were other greats in his own time, like Langford and Jeannette. But the heavyweight championship was open only to whites. Black fighters George Dixon, Barbados Joe Walcott, and Joe Gans had won titles at

In a famous bout with former heavyweight champ Jim Jeffries, Johnson (right) holds his ground. Jeffries tries his "crouch" which had destroyed so many other opponents Nevertheless, Johnson pounded Jeffries in this fight.

lower weights, but blacks could not get a chance at the world heavyweight title.

World champion Jim Jeffries, who had never been knocked down or defeated, retired from the ring in 1904, and Marvin Hart was proclaimed champion. Two years later, Canadian Tommy Burns beat Hart and took the title. Jack Johnson challenged Burns, but the new champion was busy defending his title in Europe and Australia. In Australia, a promoter finally persuaded Burns to meet Johnson's challenge for a guarantee of $30,000. As the challenger, Johnson was guaranteed $5000. At 6 feet, Johnson was five inches taller than Burns and 20 pounds heavier. Burns was a game fighter, but he was unable to land a single hard punch. Johnson became the new heavyweight champion.

After appearing on the stage and in a few exhibition bouts, Johnson took on Stanley Ketchel, the middleweight champion. They agreed the bout should go the 20-round limit because it was being filmed. But in the 12th round, Ketchel threw a sudden right that dropped the champion. Johnson bounced right up and hit Ketchel squarely in the mouth with a right. Not only did that punch end the fight, but it snapped off Ketchel's front teeth at the gums.

The fact that the world heavy-

Johnson, Jack

weight champion was a proud and flashy black was intolerable to many whites. Many prominent people felt that some white boxer *must* be found to win the title back. Novelist Jack London wrote in *The New York Herald,* "Jeffries must emerge from his alfalfa farm and remove the golden smile from Johnson's face. Jeff, it's up to you."

Jeffries was happy in retirement, but he yielded to the pressure. Jeffries went into training and lost 90 pounds—down to his fighting weight of 227. But he was 35 years old and had been in retirement for six years. Jack Johnson was 26 and in his prime.

In the 15th round, Johnson knocked Jeffries down—something no one had ever done before.

The defeat of the "Great White Hope" by the laughing, bragging Johnson caused rioting in several cities. A total of 19 people died in the first major American interracial violence since Civil War days.

In 1912, Johnson was charged with violating the Mann Act, which prohibits the transportation of women across state lines for immoral purposes. His two marriages to white women had angered authorities. To avoid prison, Johnson fled to Europe. He later lived in Argentina and Havana, Cuba.

In Havana, Johnson, now 37, fought 250-pound Jess Willard. Johnson lost the heavyweight title after 26 rounds, fought in 105-degree heat. The search for the "Great White Hope" was ended.

After his 1915 defeat in Havana, Johnson continued to live high. In Spain, he boxed and wrestled, acted in a movie, and tried bullfighting. In 1919, he moved to Mexico. A year later, he returned to the United States and was arrested for the earlier violation of the Mann Act. His plea for a reduced sentence was turned down, and Johnson served 11 months in prison.

Freed in 1921, Johnson did some exhibition boxing, appeared in vaudeville, and did some preaching. He was ignored by the newspapers, except for his frequent arrests for speeding. Johnson always drove a late-model Lincoln. "I must confess a weakness for fast driving," he said. It was a fatal weakness.

On June 10, 1946, while driving to New York after a Texas circus appearance, Johnson's car left the road near Raleigh, North Carolina, and struck a pole. He died three hours later. So ended the life of Jack Johnson.

There were 2500 mourners at his funeral in Chicago. Nat Fleischer, one of the sport's greatest authorities, said in 1927, "I have no hesitation in naming Jack Johnson as the greatest of them all."

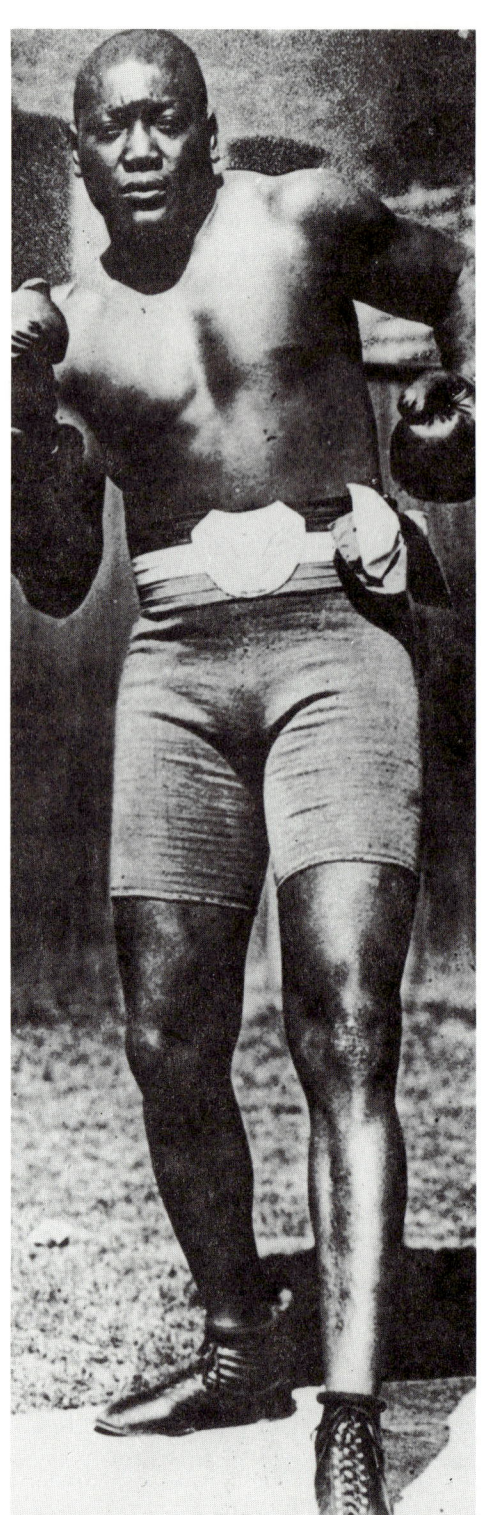

Jack Johnson was an awesome figure in the ring. Here he displays his heavyweight championship belt.

Johnson shakes hands with Jim Flynn before a bout.

Johnson connects with a hard right to the jaw of Jess Willard in their title fight in 1915. In the 26th round, Willard floored Johnson for the title. The fight took place in Havana, Cuba, and when Johnson lost, he returned to the United States.

Johnson was a powerful and controversial fighter. Long after his career was over, a Broadway play was produced about him called "The Great White Hope." Johnson's popularity was never as high during his lifetime as it was when this play was first seen.

After he lost his title and served a jail sentence, Johnson boxed in many exhibition matches throughout America.

Johnson, Rafer (1934-),

decathlon champion, was born in Hillsboro, Texas. One of six children, Johnson grew up in Kingsburg, California. As a high schooler, he excelled not only in track events but in football, basketball, and baseball as well. Concentrating on the decathlon at 16, Johnson won two state meets for high schoolers. He earned a scholarship to the University of California at Los Angeles (UCLA). At 19, he got his first taste of international competition when he won the decathlon at the Pan-American Games. In

1955, Johnson broke Bob Mathias' world record at the National Amateur Athletic Union (AAU) championship. After placing second in the decathlon at the 1956 Olympics, Johnson won the gold medal in the 1960 Games at Rome, Italy. Having achieved this feat, he retired from competition. He remained in the public's eye for his acting skills and public service.

In the 1948 Olympics, a 17-year-old schoolboy named Bob Mathias stunned the world by winning the decathlon. Some said there would never be another like him. The versatile young athlete from little Tulare, California, had come out of nowhere to conquer the world's greatest athletes. He did it again in 1952—and then almost everyone believed there would never be another like him.

But while Bob Mathias was winning his second Olympic gold medal, "another one like him" was growing up just 30 miles down the road from Tulare in the little farm town of Kingsburg. Rafer Lewis Johnson was only 16 when he watched Mathias compete in Tulare in 1952. Mathias broke the world decathlon record that day, and he deeply impressed Rafer Johnson. But the rest of the decathloners did not. There were 26 contestants, and Rafer told his coach—honestly but not brashly—"I think I could have beaten most of them."

At 15, Rafer had long-jumped more than 21 feet. He was also a fine sprinter and hurdler, and he would soon become a football and basketball star. Young Johnson played baseball, too, and batted .500 one year. Johnson takes due credit for his success in track, football, and basketball, but he says he hit .500 that year only because "I was so fast I could beat out a lot of slow-rollers."

The meet he saw at Tulare got Rafer interested in the decathlon in addition to his other sports. He won two state high school decathlon meets. He began to prepare for more and more events. He could run the hurdles in 14.3 seconds; high-jump 6 feet, 3 inches; throw the 12-pound high school shot almost 52 feet; and long-jump 23 feet. In the discus, he was only 10 feet short of Al Oerter's national high school record.

In 1954, Rafer Johnson was a high school senior. He entered the Amateur Athletic Union (AAU) national decathlon meet in Atlantic City, New Jersey. He still had some events to straighten out—such as the pole vault, the javelin, and the

After the awards ceremony at the 1960 Olympics, Johnson (middle), winner of the decathlon, shakes hands with C. K. Yang (left), the second-place finisher, and Vasily Kuznetsov, the bronze medal winner.

Johnson, Rafer

Proudly carrying the American flag, Rafer leads the U.S. squad into the stadium in Rome before the 1960 Olympics.

Soaring through the air, Johnson jumps 24 feet, 1 3/8 inches in the long-jump event of the 1960 Olympic decathlon.

1500-meter run—but he finished third. Bob Richards won the meet, helped by a pole vault of over 15 feet.

But Rafer Johnson had the incentive he needed. He entered the University of California at Los Angeles (UCLA) that fall. He was intent on going after the world decathlon record.

Rafer Johnson was born on August 18, 1934, in Hillsboro, Texas. He was the son of a poor black couple who were trying to raise their six children well in spite of segregation and poverty. The family moved to Kingsburg, California. Rafer's brother Jimmy became a fine athlete, too. Jimmy went to UCLA and starred in football and track. Later, he became an All-Pro cornerback for the San Francisco 49'ers.

Rafer not only excelled in sports. He was also an "A" student and the president of his high school class. UCLA was getting more than just a fine athlete.

As a freshman at UCLA, Rafer played basketball for coach John Wooden and then joined coach Ducky Drake's track team. Ducky Drake had once run the half-mile, mile, two-mile, and relay in the same day's track meet. Drake expected hard work from his track team. Rafer started fast. He tied the national freshman hurdles record at 14 seconds flat. In the 1955 season, he was the fastest low-hurdler in the country. He won six events in one dual meet.

The 6-foot, 3-inch, 190-pound all-round athlete kept on winning. Later in 1955, Johnson was the surprise 19-year-old winner of the Pan-American Games. He was competing against the best decathloners of the Western Hemisphere. His point total was near that of the world decathlon champion, Russia's Vasily Kuznetsov. On June 10 and 11, 1955, Kingsburg was host to the National AAU decathlon contest. Rafer Johnson put out his greatest effort. He broke Bob Mathias' world record by 98 points. With a little improvement in the high jump, the pole vault and the 1500 meters, it was obvious that

During one of the grueling decathlon events, Johnson puts the shot en route to his gold medal victory in the event at the 1960 Olympics.

Johnson competes in the 1956 Olympics, throwing the discus in the decathlon competition.

Rafer successfully clears the bar in the pole-vault portion of the decathlon at the 1956 Melbourne, Australia, Olympics.

Johnson might become the Olympic champion the next year.

In Russia, Kuznetsov broke his own world record a few months later.

As a sophomore in 1956, Rafer Johnson competed in varsity track with distinction. He scored 16 points in the Pacific Coast Conference (now the Pac-8) meet. His score helped UCLA defeat its bitter rival, the University of Southern California (USC), for the first time. Johnson was long-jumping over 25 feet and hurdling in 13.8 seconds. He led UCLA to the National Collegiate Athletic Association (NCAA) title.

Johnson made the 1956 Olympic team as both a decathloner and a long jumper. At the Olympic Games in Melbourne, Australia, he began to have knee problems. His bad knee got worse, and he withdrew from the long jump. The injury probably cost him first place in the decathlon. He finished second, for a silver medal, behind his teammate Milt Campbell.

In the next two years, Johnson dueled with Kuznetsov for the world record in the decathlon. Kuznetsov took it in 1958, but Johnson got it back that same year in a head-to-head battle in Moscow. Then, Kuznetsov regained the record in 1959.

A great 1960 Olympic battle seemed to be shaping up between the two. But Johnson was in an auto accident, and his back was badly injured. For a year and a half he could not train. Johnson then began coaching another UCLA student, C. K. Yang, a native of Nationalist China (Taiwan). Yang became one of the world's best and a potential Olympic gold medalist.

Johnson was back in shape in time for the 1960 Games at Rome, Italy. Now he was a powerful 198 pounds and a mature 26 years old. He was ready to take on the world. Johnson had won so much respect from his U.S. teammates that he was chosen to carry the American flag into Rome's Stadio Olimpico for the opening ceremonies. "I'm

Johnson, Rafer

Johnson holds some of the equipment he used to compete in the decathlon —the shot, javelin, and discus.

Rafer Johnson receives the 1958 Sportsman of the Year trophy given by Sports Illustrated. *Here, the magazine's managing editor, Sidney James, presents Johnson with a replica of an ancient Grecian urn for his athletic feats.*

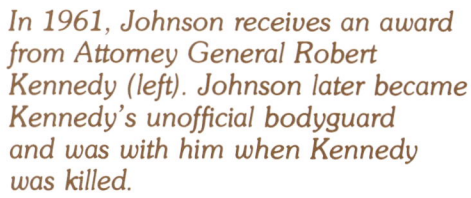

In 1961, Johnson receives an award from Attorney General Robert Kennedy (left). Johnson later became Kennedy's unofficial bodyguard and was with him when Kennedy was killed.

Johnson wins his heat of the 100-meter dash event in the decathlon during the 1960 Rome Olympics.

prepared to win, whatever it takes," said Rafer.

For two days, Johnson, Yang, and Kuznetsov matched their speed, their strength, and their stamina. All three were marvelous, but Johnson's greater strength helped him in the weight events. He threw the shot 51 feet, 10¾ inches. He was far ahead in the discus and a little ahead in the javelin. But Yang, who had learned to hurdle and sprint with Rafer, was getting the edge in the ground events.

The competition settled down to the 10th and last event—the grueling 1500-meter race. Rafer hated that event, which is just short of a mile. But he had to keep within 10 seconds of Yang to stay ahead of him in total points. Johnson stuck with Yang as though it were a matter of life and death. He finished only 1.2 seconds behind. He had clinched the gold medal. Johnson embraced C. K. Yang. "I wanted that win real bad," Rafer said. "But I never want to go through that again—never. Tonight I'm going for a walk for about four hours and look at the moon. I don't know where—just walk, walk, walk. I've got to unwind. I'm through, man, through."

Rafer Johnson never competed in the decathlon again. But he went on to make a name for himself in acting, public service, and other fields.

⚾ Johnson, Walter (1887-1946),

baseball player, was born in Humboldt, Kansas. Moving with his family to California, he started his career in baseball early. While working and pitching for the Weiser Idaho Telephone Company in 1906, Johnson signed to play with the Washington Senators. In 1913, he won the American League Most-Valuable-Player (MVP) award, finishing the season with a 36-7 won-lost record, 12 shutouts, and a 1.14 earned-run average (ERA). In 1924, Johnson finished with a 23-7 record and an ERA of 2.72, which earned him his second MVP award. Winning 20 or more games in 12 seasons and more than 30 games in two of those seasons, Johnson ranks first in major-league shutouts (113), first in strikeouts (3508), second in career victories (416), and first in lifetime ERA (2.37). He served as manager of the Senators from 1929 to 1932 and of the Cleveland Indians in 1933. After suffering from a brain tumor for nearly eight months, Johnson died in 1946. Known as "The Big Train," Walter Johnson was one of the first five players named to the Baseball Hall of Fame in 1936.

The record book has a list a mile long when it comes to the accomplishments of "The Big Train," Walter Johnson.

Johnson played with the Washington Senators from 1907 through 1927 when they were often as bad as noted in the popular saying, "first in war, first in peace, and last in the American League." Yet Johnson had more victories (416) than any other American League pitcher in history. He ranks second only to the great Cy Young (511) on the all-time list. Johnson stands alone in career strikeouts (3508) and shutouts (113). His nearest rivals in those categories are Grover Cleveland Alexander with 90 shutouts and Bob Gibson with 3117 strikeouts. Johnson also compiled a lifetime earned-run average (ERA) of 2.37, first on the all-time list.

Walter Perry Johnson was born November 6, 1887, in Humboldt, Kansas. Soon after his birth, his family moved to California. There, he began his baseball career as a strong-armed catcher for the Oil Field Juniors. Johnson would have been a pitcher right from the start, but no one on the team could catch his bullet-like deliveries.

At 16, he was pitching and digging holes for the Weiser Idaho Telephone Company. That year (1906) catcher Cliff Blankenship, on a scouting mission for the Washington Senators, signed him for $350 a month with expenses and a $100 bonus. And in August of the

During his major-league career, Walter Johnson hurled a total of 5924 innings.

following year, Johnson made his major-league debut with the Senators.

He pitched his first game against the mighty Detroit Tigers and was in the lead until the eighth inning. After that inning, Tiger Ty Cobb beat out a bunt, raced to third on another bunt, and then scored the winning run. But even though the Senators lost that game, Johnson's blazing fast ball gained respect —even from Cobb. The young hurler from the California oil hills was in the big leagues to stay.

Johnson's first partial season with the Senators produced only a 5-9 record, including two shutouts. His second- and third-season records (14-14 and 13-25) were also below par for him. But in 1910, he began to click. Johnson started a remarkable string of 20-plus win seasons. By 1919, he reached 10 straight years with 20 or more wins and was rated as the best right-hander in baseball. The won-lost records during those 10 years are amazing—25-17, 23-15, 32-12, 36-7, 28-18, 27-13, 25-20, 23-16, 23-13, and 20-14.

During his prime years, Johnson pitched many low-hit games— including five one-hitters in 1913, the year he won his first Most-Valuable-Player (MVP) award. But his only no-hitter came in 1920, a season that was slowed to an 8-10 record by a sore arm. On July 1, he pitched the 1-0 classic against the Boston Red Sox.

A problem in pitching for Washington was the lower salaries Senator players received compared to the rest of the league. Operating on a small budget, Senator's owner

37

Johnson, Walter

Retiring from the mound, Walter Johnson picks up the microphone to broadcast home games of the Washington Senators in 1939.

Johnson (left) shakes hands with the famous owner of the Philadelphia Athletics, Connie Mack, before a big game.

Clark Griffith could not afford to be overly generous—even to a star like Walter Johnson. In 1913, Johnson turned in his second straight season of more than 30 victories with a record of 36-7—including 12 shutouts and five one-hitters. Walter Johnson felt he merited a larger salary than the $12,000 he was then being paid.

Yet it was not until the following year that he threatened to leave Washington. At that time, a newly formed Federal League was providing competition for the services of major-league players.

The Federal League's Chicago club offered Johnson $16,000 and a $10,000 bonus to play with them. Clark Griffith agreed to raise Walter Johnson's salary with the Senators to $16,000, but the Washington board of directors refused a $10,000 bonus to match Chicago. Only because of his wife's love for Washington did Johnson agree to stay with the Senators. Then through a surprising event, he did receive the extra $10,000. The owner of the American League's Chicago franchise, Charles Comiskey, dashed off a $10,000 check to insure that Johnson would not move to Chicago.

In 1924, when he was nearing 37, it seemed that Walter Johnson was finally getting tired. He had not reached his usual 20-game mark in four seasons. Then he surprised everyone by coming back to post an astonishing 23-7 record—leading the American League in victories, winning percentage, shutouts (6), strikeouts (158), and earned-run average (2.72). For his achievements he was given his second MVP award.

That year was very significant to Washington baseball. Bucky Harris, the "boy wonder" manager, guided the Senators to the American League pennant and then on to a World Series victory over John

Taking over the managing job of the Cleveland Indians in 1933, Johnson talks with his men before a game.

McGraw's New York Giants. Walter Johnson won the decisive seventh game of the series for the Senators.

Clark Griffith credited Johnson's 22 scoreless innings against the strong Philadelphia Athletics in 1912 as his greatest feat. Yet Johnson felt differently. He rated his opening-day appearance in 1926 as his best. He was, by that time, old for a pitcher. But he went 15 innings to beat the A's and their best pitcher, Eddie Rommel, 1-0.

Johnson's pitching feats were endless. Even backed by a weak team, he was involved in 64 1-0 decisions—and 38 times he was the winner in those games.

A broken leg from a line drive off the bat of roommate Joe Judge finally put an end to Johnson's career. The accident occurred during spring training in 1927. Hindered by the injury, Johnson had a poor 5-6 record that year. The following spring Johnson lost 35 pounds after a severe bout of influenza. "The Big Train" was finished.

In 1929, Johnson replaced Bucky Harris as manager of the Senators. His four seasons as skipper were marked with defeat. He also seemed more impatient than usual. In 1933, he drifted over to Cleveland as manager. There he was considered cold and surly by many of his players. The change may have been caused by the death of his 36-year-old wife in 1930, leaving him with five children to raise.

In 1936, Walter Johnson was one of the first five men named to the Baseball Hall of Fame. The honor came to a man who had shown fine pitching through the years. Some experts even say he was the best hurler in history.

In 1946, Johnson was stricken with a brain tumor. He died on December 10 at the age of 59.

Jones, Bert (1951-),

football player, was born in Ruston, Louisiana. He is the son of former pro football star Dub Jones. With his father's encouragement, coaching, and connections, Bert had an opportunity afforded to few youngsters. A local winner in the annual Punt, Pass, and Kick contest, he later became an outstanding quarterback in high school. Jones then attended Louisiana State University, where he passed for 28 touchdowns in three years. He was an All-America selection and *The Sporting News'* College Player of the Year in 1972. Jones was chosen in the first round of the 1973 National Football League (NFL) draft by the Baltimore Colts. In his second season, 1974, he set a league record of 17 straight completions in one game. In 1976, Jones had one of the greatest seasons by an NFL quarterback. He completed 60.3 per cent of his passes for 3104 yards and 24 touchdowns. He was named the NFL's Most Valuable Player that year.

Being the son of a famous athlete has certain advantages. High school quarterback Bert Jones used to spend his summers as ball boy at the Cleveland Browns' training camp. Bert got the job through his father, Dub Jones, who used to play for the Browns. Bert would warm up with the players and get tips from star quarterbacks like Frank Ryan.

But there are disadvantages, too. One is living up to the father's reputation.

Bertram Hays Jones was born September 1, 1951, in Ruston, Louisiana. Two months later, his father Dub scored six touchdowns in a game between the Browns and the Chicago Bears. That tied a National Football League (NFL) record that has yet to be broken.

Until December 15, 1974, no father and son had ever been listed in the NFL record book at the same time. On that day, Bert Jones lived up to his father's reputation. He set a remarkable record by completing 17 consecutive passes in a game against the New York Jets.

That same day, young Jones of the Baltimore Colts also set team records for most completions (36) and most attempts (53) in a game. He also passed for four touchdowns and 385 yards in the Colts' victory.

Although it was the last game of the 1974 season, it was the game that started Jones on his way to superstardom. The training that Bert Jones received in his youth had a lot to do with his fast rise to the top.

After his birth, Bert was handicapped by a bone problem in his

One of the strongest quarterbacks in the NFL, Bert Jones sets up to throw a long one.

40

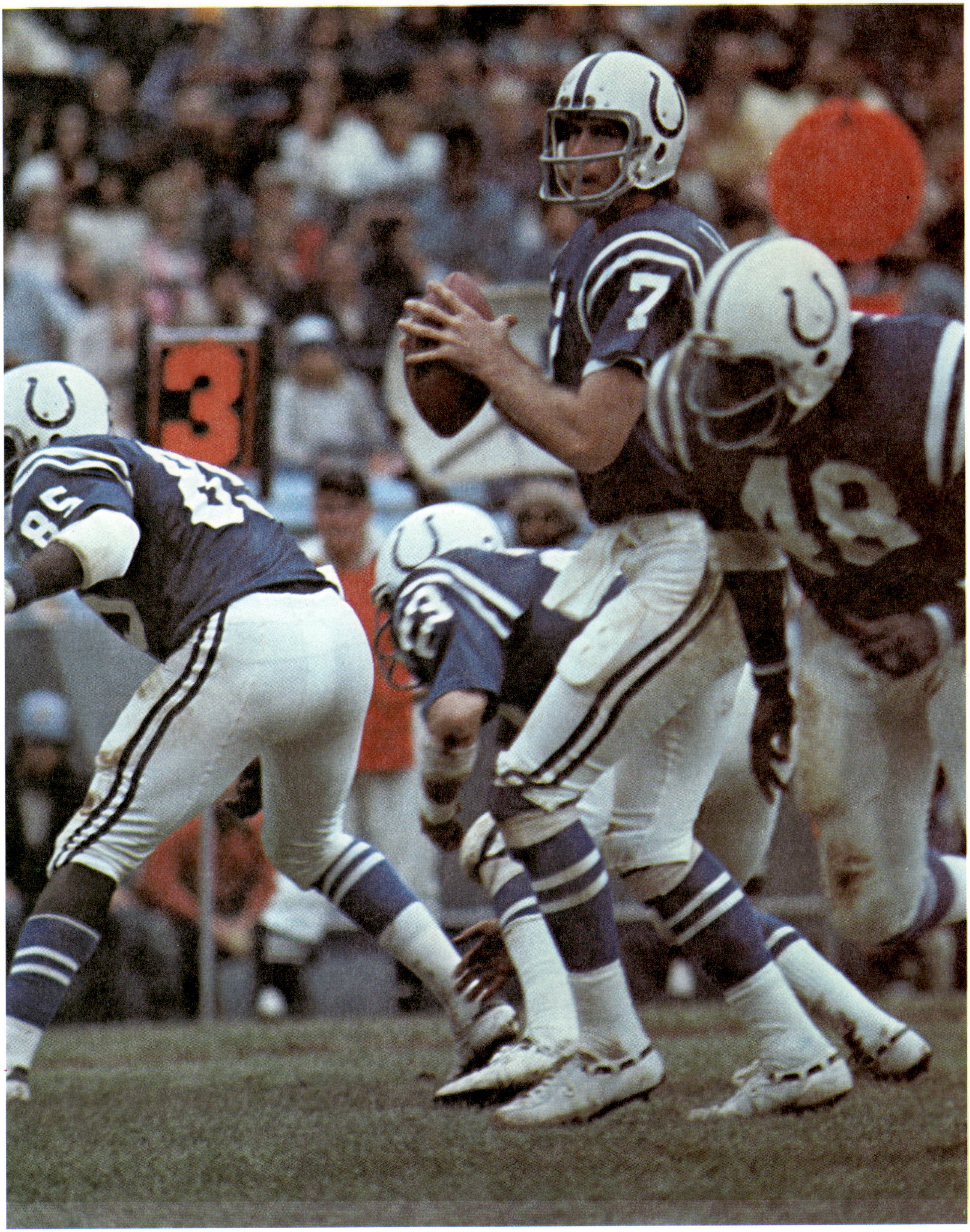

Jones, Bert

foot. He had to wear a brace much of the time until he was four. But he made up for being slow-footed by throwing things.

Growing up in Ruston, Bert learned early that he would have to make sacrifices to be a good football player. He was a fine baseball player for an American Legion championship team, but he later gave it up because he did not want to divert his attention from football.

By his senior year in high school, Jones was an outstanding quarterback. He was recruited by many colleges and decided to attend Louisiana State University.

During his college career, Bert became famous as the son of Dub Jones. In three years, he passed for 28 touchdowns, ran for eight, and completed 52.6 per cent of his passes. Throwing 14 touchdown passes as a senior, Jones was chosen by *The Sporting News* as College Player of the Year. He was a consensus All-American that year.

In 1973, the Baltimore Colts were just one of many pro teams interested in Bert Jones. The Colts were willing to make a major trade to get his draft rights. "I knew when we got the chance to draft Jones with New Orleans' choice [which Baltimore traded for] that we had the best quarterback talent to come out of college in the last 20 years," said Joe Thomas, general manager of the Colts.

Louisiana State University's Bert Jones dances in for a touchdown during the 1971 Sun Bowl. Jones, who threw three touchdown passes, quarterbacked his club to a 33-15 victory and was selected the game's Most Valuable Player.

The Colts went through some of the toughest seasons in their history in 1973 and 1974—Bert's first two seasons in the NFL. But they were willing to go with the young quarterback.

Baltimore started him for the first five games of his rookie season. But team problems, along with problems of his own, kept Bert on the bench for six of the 14 regular-season games. The next year, he started for most of the season, but it did not help the Colts. They won only one of their first 13 games.

Then came the contest against the New York Jets to close out the season. Bert hit on 17 straight passes. He also wiped out Johnny Unitas' team records for most passes attempted and completed. The strong-armed Jones finished the season with a 53 per cent completion rate.

In 1975, Bert Jones was Baltimore's main man. That season, he broke another Unitas record by completing 59 per cent of his passes. In his final 10 games, the 6-foot, 3-inch, 210-pound quarterback was intercepted only four times. He put together another long completion streak of 12 and had touchdown throws of 89 and 90 yards to Roger Carr. The Jones-Carr combination quickly became one of the most dangerous passing threats in the league. Jones ranked fourth in the NFL in passing, even though he played half the season with broken ribs.

In 1976, Bert Jones had one of the finest seasons by an NFL quarterback. He completed over 60 per cent of his passes for 24 touchdowns and a league-leading 3104 yards.

More important, he turned his team around. With a record of 10-4, the Colts made the playoffs. They had come a long way from their disastrous 2-12 season in 1974.

When he was not playing football, Jones took part in a variety of pastimes. He enjoyed hunting, skiing, and scuba diving. He shot golf in the low 70's and flew his own plane.

On the playing field, Jones possessed great leadership qualities. "Bert's the type of guy who wants to give you that old country boy approach, but underneath it all he is one smart cookie," said George Kunz, his teammate, friend, and key blocker.

In 1976, Bert Jones was amazing. He completed 60.3 per cent of his passes for 3104 yards. He tossed 24 touchdown strikes and had only eight of his passes intercepted all year. The Colts were 11-3 and made the playoffs again. He was recognized for his banner season in being selected the NFL's Most Valuable Player.

After another fine performance in 1977, Jones was plagued with shoulder injuries the next two seasons. Still, he ranked sixth among pro football's all-time passers by 1980. Joe Namath, one of the game's greats, called Bert Jones the best quarterback in football. Others would agree.

Jones, Bobby (1902-1971),

golfer, was born in Atlanta, Georgia, the son of a noted lawyer. Taking up golf at the age of five, Jones entered his first U.S. Amateur championship in 1916. Then only 14 years old, he stunned everyone by leading the field in the first qualifying round. In 1923, he won his first major tournament, the National Open. For the next eight years Jones was the dominant force in the game, winning 13 major championships. His best year was 1930, when he captured the Grand Slam with victories in the British Amateur, the British Open, the U.S. Open, and the U.S. Amateur. That same year, Jones laid plans for a golf course to be built near Augusta, Georgia. This famous course is now the site of the Masters tournament, one of the most prestigious events on the golf tour. Suffering from back problems, Jones played little throughout the 1930's. He quit for good in 1948, when he was stricken with a crippling nerve illness. Bobby Jones will always remain a legendary figure in the game of golf.

Bobby Jones retired from tournament golf at 28. Yet before he retired, he earned a lasting place in sports history. He was the first to sweep golf's Grand Slam—winning the amateur and open titles of both the United States and Britain.

Jones was also proud of another accomplishment. He established the Augusta (Georgia) National Golf Club, where the U.S. Masters is played. But all his achievements were not just in golf. Bobby Jones was a scholar, too, holding degrees in engineering, law, and English literature.

Robert Tyre Jones, Jr., was born on St. Patrick's Day, March 17, 1902, in Atlanta, Georgia. Living near Atlanta's East Lake golf course, young Bobby would often go to watch the club pro, Stewart Maiden, coach his pupils. Then, carefully imitating the swings, the boy would practice what he had seen. He was only five when he began playing the course.

During the summer of 1916, 14-year-old Bobby Jones took part in the U.S. Amateur tournament held at the Merion Cricket Club in Philadelphia. Surprisingly, he led the field in the first qualifying round. Even then he was smashing 250-yard drives.

His first match was against Eben Byers, a former amateur champion. The sportswriter Grantland Rice wrote of an incident from the match:

"Byers was straight down the middle. Jones hooked way off the fairway into deep rough. After a short delay, Byers hit his second shot and started walking ahead.

"Jones, deep in the morass, called out, 'Fore, Mr. Byers!'

"'I'm sorry,' Byers responded. 'I thought you had picked up

Jones putts at the 1934 Masters invitational tourney in Augusta, Georgia.

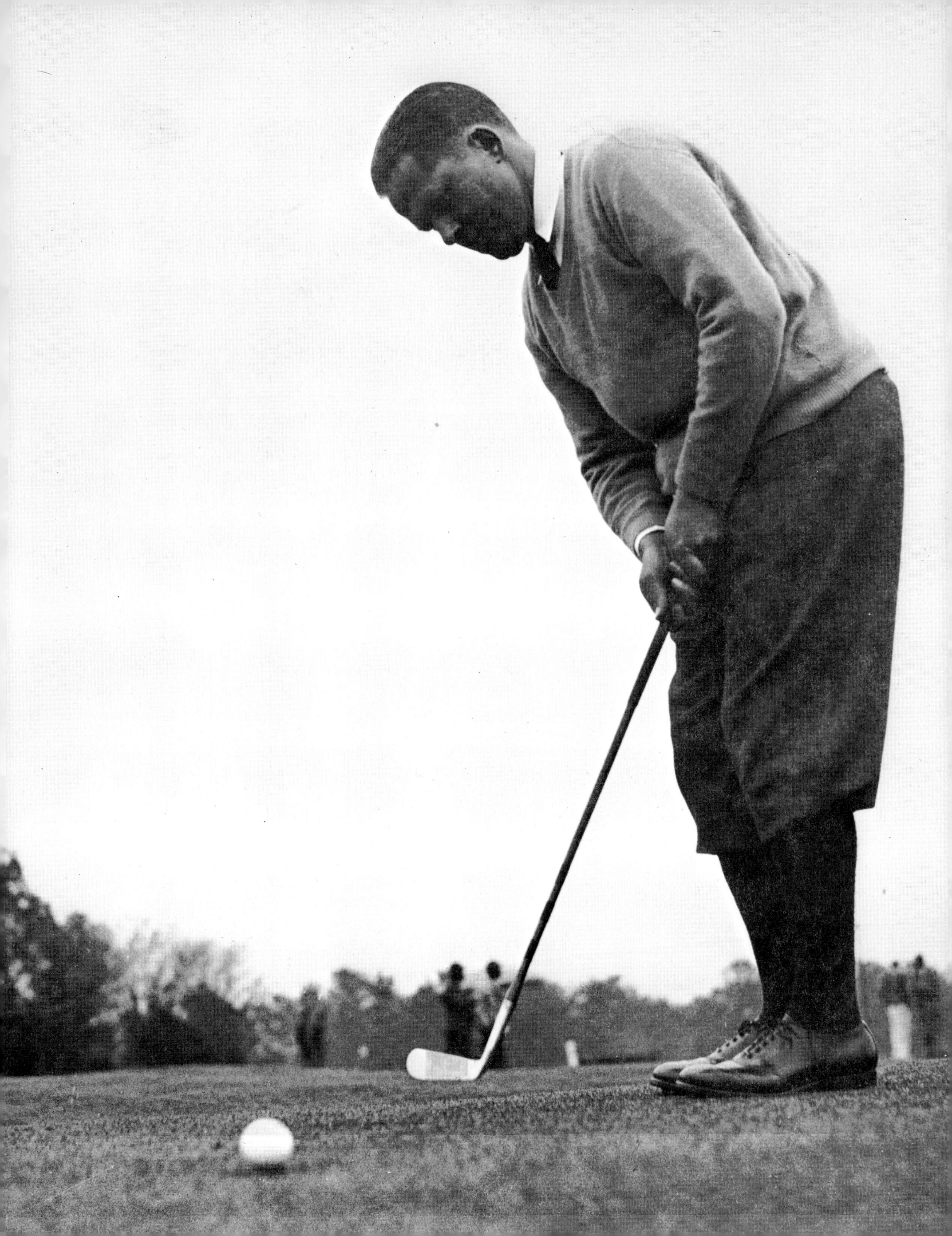

Jones, Bobby

Sending up a spray of sand, Jones blasts out of a bunker at the 1930 British Amateur in Scotland.

In 1932, Bobby Jones' lifelong dream of building a perfect golf course was becoming reality. Here Jones (left) discusses construction with the superintendent of the project which would become the new Augusta National golf course in Augusta, Georgia.

[taken a penalty stroke to get out of the rough].'

"'Picked up hell!' fired Jones. 'You just watch this one.'

"The recovery shot stopped about four feet from the cup for a birdie 3. That was a large measure of satisfaction for the hot-blooded Georgia kid." Bobby Jones won.

Jones also won his second match. In the third round, he faced defending champion Bob Gardner. They made a strange twosome. Gardner, a former pole-vault record-holder, was a well-built 6-footer. Bobby Jones was then a pudgy boy, standing only 5 feet, 4 inches and weighing 170 pounds. For his footwear, Jones had screwed spikes into the bottom of a pair of army shoes. Outmatched, Bobby Jones lost the round.

Through his teens, he fought two foes—his temper and his big appetite. When things went wrong with his game, he usually flung his clubs away. And unlike other players who skipped the noon meal, Jones always enjoyed a big lunch, topped off by pie à la mode. But by the early 1920's he had reformed. He worked to curb his temper, and for lunch he had crackers and milk.

During the 1923 U.S. Open at Inwood Country Club on Long Island, the 20-year-old Jones defeated Bobby Cruikshank in a playoff. For the next eight years he completely dominated the game.

During this time, the gifted Jones sought other achievements. He graduated in engineering from Georgia Technological Institute, went through Harvard Law School, and later obtained a law degree at Emory University in Atlanta.

Bobby Jones' popularity soared in 1926 when he became the first amateur in 29 years to win the British Open. His smiling face became well known after photographs of him appeared often in newspaper columns.

Still playing as an amateur, Jones beat other amateurs and pros alike. His titles included five U.S. Amateurs, four U.S. Opens, three British Opens, and one British Amateur—the tournaments that made up the Grand Slam. In 1930, Jones became the first golfer to win all four events in one year.

He had no more worlds to conquer as an amateur, so he then accepted a contract for making films on golf—finally he had become a pro.

In the early 1930's, Bobby Jones joined his father in a land investment and development business, operating largely in Florida. His business ventures, coupled with back troubles, cost him much of his fairway skill. Jones began to concentrate on his law practice in Atlanta.

Still, he continued to appear in selected tournaments until 1948, when he was stricken by a crippling nerve affliction that eventually put him in a wheelchair.

In one of his real estate deals,

A promising young amateur in 1917, Jones takes a swing at the Western Amateur championships.

Driving off the third tee, Bobby Jones is about to win the U.S. Amateur title and complete his Grand Slam victory in 1930.

Jones found a beautiful tree nursery covering 365 acres of woodlands near Augusta. The area gave him an idea, and at once he began planning a golf course for the site. The course was designed to be "playable" for casual golfers, yet to present a challenge for the more serious. In 1934, an informal tournament, the Masters, was held for

Jones, Bobby

U.S. President Dwight Eisenhower, a golfer himself, presents Bobby Jones with a portrait he painted of the former Grand Slam winner.

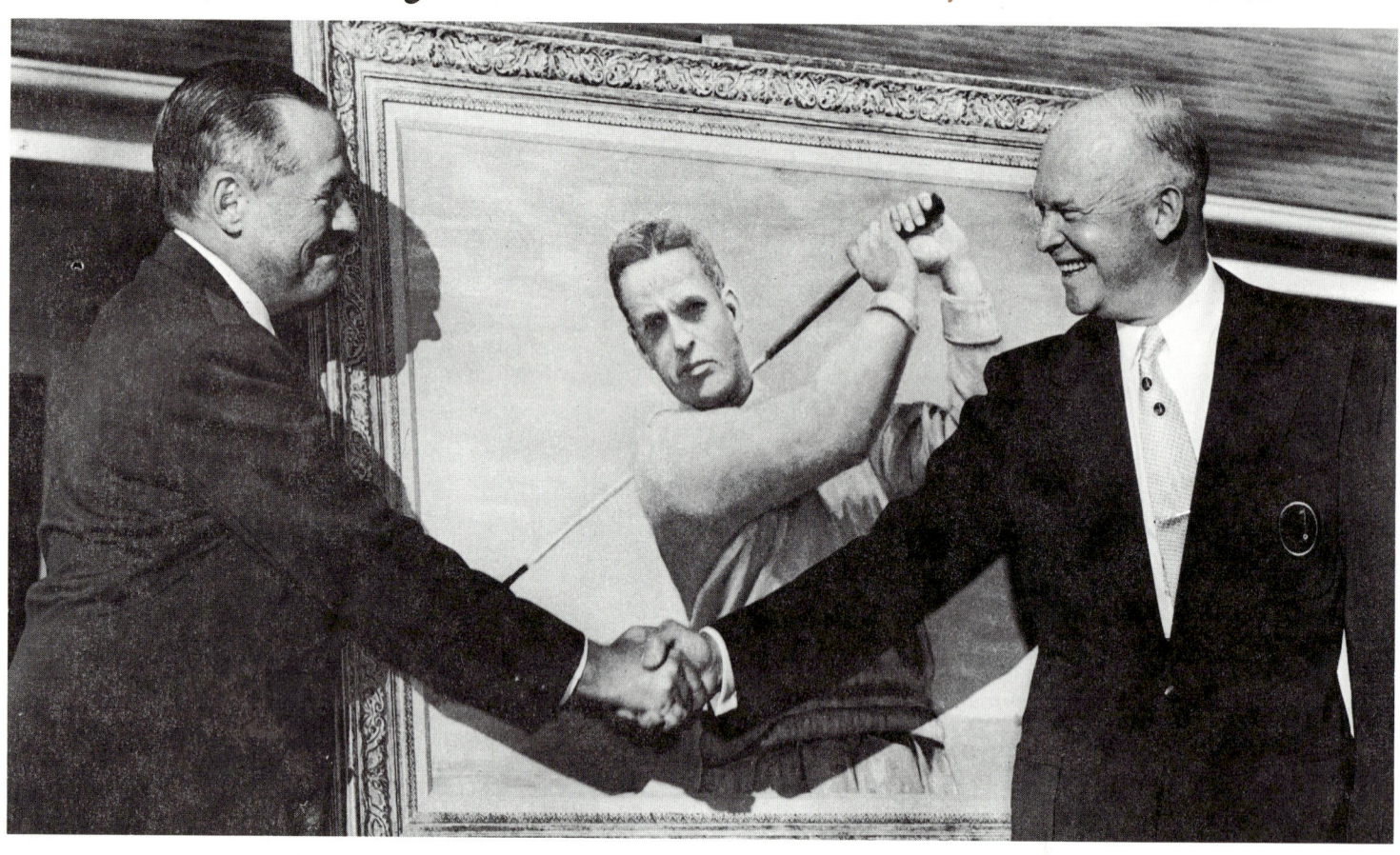

During World War II, Jones left his clubs for a while and served in the U.S. Army Air Corps.

the leading golfers of the time. Today, it is one of the major championships in the world and an important part of the modern Grand Slam (the British and U.S. Opens, the PGA Championship, and the Masters).

The Masters will always remain a memorial to Bobby Jones, the greatest amateur golfer of all time.

Jones married in 1924 and became the father of three children. He served as a lieutenant colonel in World War II. After the war, he was active in the Republican party and served as a fund-raiser for Dwight D. Eisenhower's election campaign. Jones and Eisenhower became good friends and often golfed together in Augusta.

On December 18, 1971, after suffering for more than 20 years, Bobby Jones died.

Acclaimed as a conquering hero, Bobby rides down Broadway in New York following his return from England in 1930. While in England, he captured both the British Open and British Amateur titles to complete a Grand Slam.

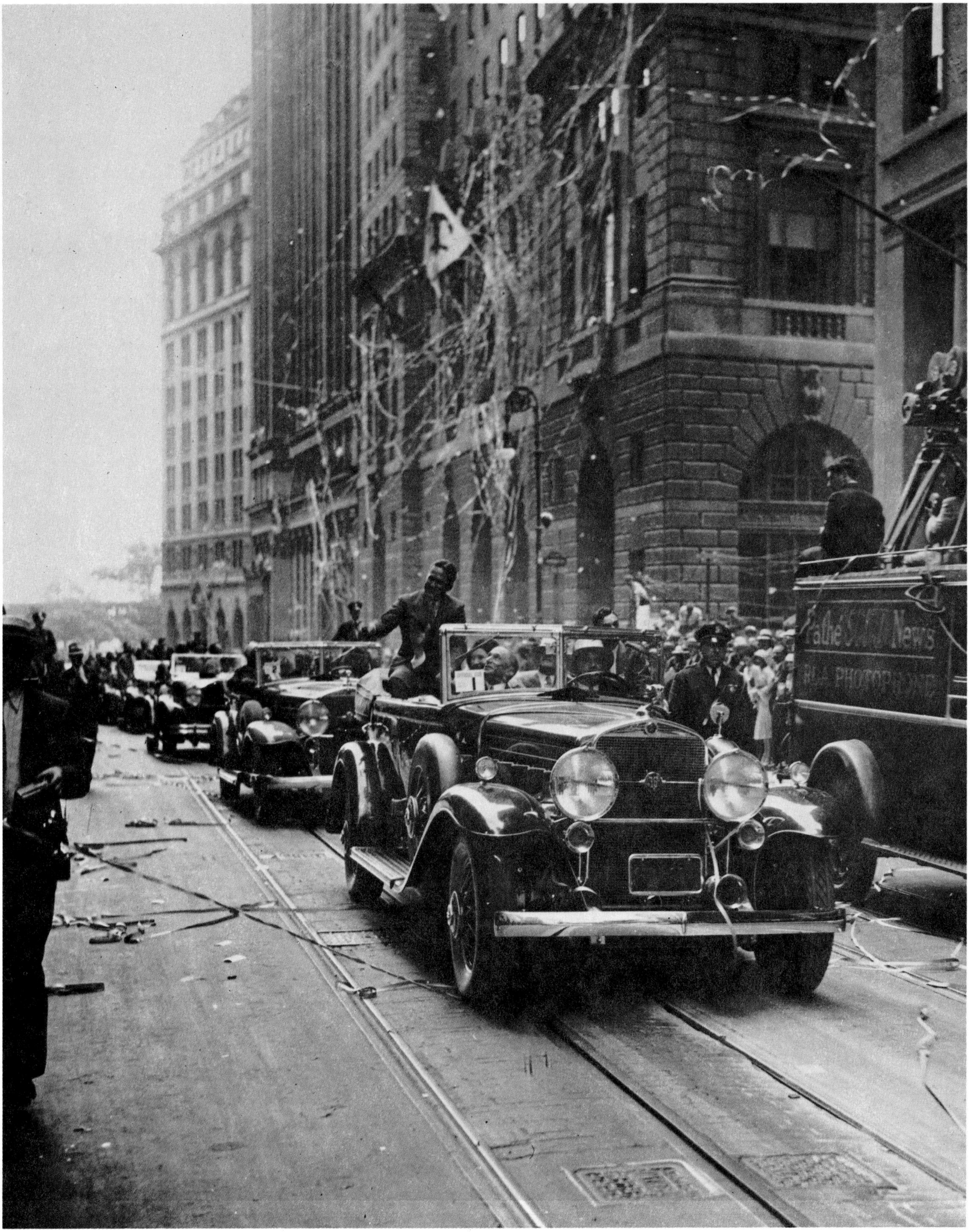
News

Jones, Deacon (David) (1938-),

football player, was born in Eatonville, Florida, and reared in Orlando. Life was hard for his family of 10, and Jones soon learned to apply his tall and muscular body to achieve success. At Hungerford High School, he starred in football, basketball, and track. After high school, he attended two colleges— Mississippi Vocational College and South Carolina State College. At the Carolina school, Jones was nicknamed "Deacon" when he began leading the football team in prayer. He achieved little fame in college and was drafted by the Los Angeles Rams in the 14th round in 1961. Blessed with great quickness, Deacon was a starter at defensive end in his first regular-season game. He played in 143 consecutive professional games before his streak was ended by a leg injury. By 1964, Jones had established himself as one of the premier pass-rushers in the game. In 1967 and 1968, he was named the league's top defensive player. He ended his career with the San Diego Chargers and the Washington Redskins.

David "Deacon" Jones, a 6-foot, 5-inch, 250-pound living legend, was regarded as a near-perfect defensive end.

From 1964 through 1970, the powerful defensive lineman was perhaps the best pass-rusher in pro football. He was named the top defensive player in the National Football League (NFL) in 1967 and 1968. Jones played in eight Pro Bowl games and was an All-NFL choice several times.

A durable player, Jones played in 143 straight games until he injured his leg in 1971. Jones had great dedication to football as well. In 1969, he tackled Zeke Bratkowski, Green Bay Packer quarterback, and caught his thumb in Bratkowski's helmet. His dislocated thumb bleeding, Jones ran off the field, had the thumb put back into place, ice-sprayed, and bandaged. Then he returned to the field and continued his job of breaking up the Packers' attack.

David Jones was born on December 9, 1938, in the village of Eatonville, Florida, and was raised in Orlando. His parents, Ishmael and Mattie Jones, had two other sons and five daughters.

Jones' father worked as a carpenter and gardener, but work was scarce and so was money. He passed on his great size and strength to his sons Hudson, Harold, and David. All three of the Jones brothers became outstanding football players.

Young David starred in football, basketball, and track at Orlando's Hungerford High School. He played football at Mississippi Vocational College and South Carolina State College. At the South

Clearing his way through the Baltimore Colts, Deacon Jones is about to nail the runner.

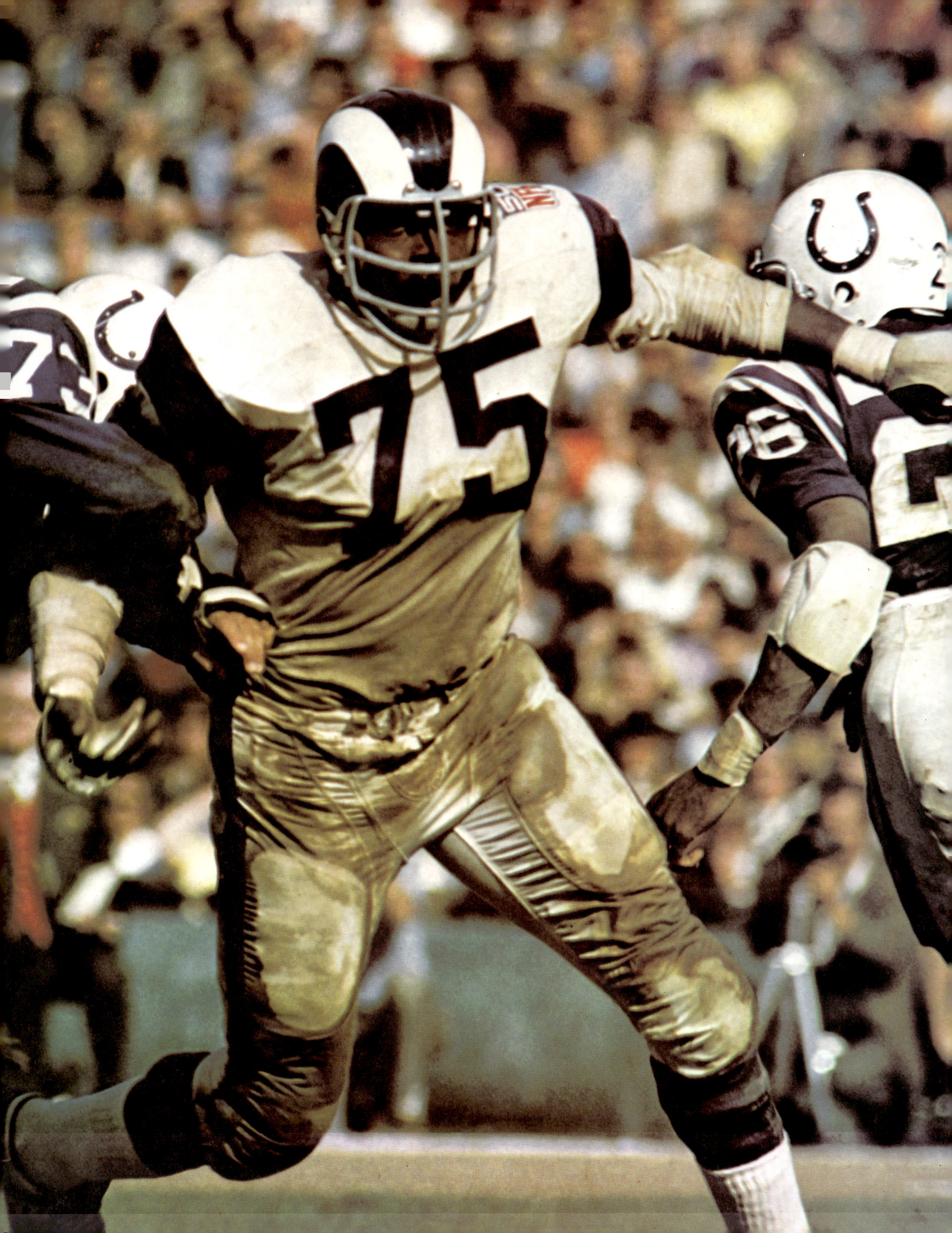
75
26

Jones, Deacon

The Los Angeles Rams' "Fearsome Foursome" move into action, led by Deacon Jones (Number 75), Merlin Olsen (Number 74), and Roger Brown (Number 78). Lamar Lundy is partially hidden behind Olsen.

Carolina school, he picked up his nickname because he led the football squad in prayer.

"I like that name," he says. "People remember it where they wouldn't remember David."

Pro scouts in those days paid little attention to black schools. But a pair of Los Angeles Ram scouts, Eddie Kotal and Johnny Sanders, noticed Jones while studying films of two backs on other teams. One big lineman kept barreling through to smother the backs' progress. The big lineman was Deacon Jones. The Rams drafted Jones in the 14th round of 1961 and signed him without a bonus.

Jones had performed as a two-way tackle through high school and college. Los Angeles already had two superb ends—Lamar Lundy and Gene Brito. So the Deacon told coach Bob Waterfield that he was an offensive tackle—a spot where the Rams were thin. Gene Brito then came down with an illness that was to prove fatal. Jones moved in as defensive end for the opening league game of 1961. He was an end for the rest of his career.

In the early days, Jones lacked skill and stamina. He loved to eat, and his weight ballooned to 290 pounds early in the 1963 season. The Rams almost traded him. Still, he came up with an occasional spectacular play. And in spite of his

Jones keeps a stuffed bear named "Herbie" buckled down in the front seat of his car as a constant companion. "Herbie" guards the car in Jones' absence.

weight, nobody could stay with him in the wind sprints. Still, Deacon thought it would be to his advantage to lose some weight. He eventually did, and his line-play greatly improved.

By 1964, Jones had put it all together. He and Merlin Olsen were operating like twin pistons on the left side. Their tightly co-ordinated running was brutal to the enemy. Along with tackle Rosey Grier and end Lamar Lundy they became known as the "Fearsome Foursome."

At the time, Gale Sayers of the Chicago Bears said, "Jones easily is the best defensive end in football. You can't run around him like you do the others because the Deacon is so quick."

Jones credited defensive end Gino Marchetti for much of his development. For years Jones studied Marchetti's moves through movies. Deacon used the Marchetti style of attack in his own game.

Enemy teams used two or more men to try to keep Jones from wrecking their plays. The Rams' answer was to use Jones as middle guard in a five-man line. This put Jones in a position to reach the enemy quarterback right away. Jones could attack so fast that he was very hard to block.

The fact that the fans regard pro players as supermen amused

An awesome figure, Jones puts an all-out rush on San Diego Charger quarterback John Hadl.

the Deacon. "The fans think that, because we're so big, we don't get hurt, that we don't suffer. But we sure do. We hurt just like ordinary folks. Sometimes I hurt so bad it brings tears to my eyes. Imagine a guy like me crying? But I do. I often play with injuries and with fever. Everybody is about equal nowadays, so you don't give any less than your very best."

"It's bad to fall on a fumble," Jones said. "It seems at least five guys always light on top of you. Once some brute landed on my spine. I couldn't get up. My legs seemed paralyzed. But the pain quickly passed. Now don't misunderstand. We're well paid for all this misery."

"Sure, David complains about being hurt," his wife Iretha said. "But he's not hard to live with as long as his teams are winning."

Off the field, Jones lived quietly. "The fast life doesn't go well with football. This is a violent sport, and you have to take care of your body to survive it. So I got married and settled down," Jones explained.

Jones later began preparing himself for an entertainment career when his playing days would be over. He took voice and acting lessons, and he cut several records, including *Loving a Pro*. Jones also headed a night-club act called "Soul by a Pro, the Deacon Jones Revue."

In 1972, Jones was traded to the San Diego Chargers. He played there for two years and then joined the Washington Redskins. After the 1974 season, he retired. Deacon Jones was inducted into the Pro Football Hall of Fame in 1980, assuring his place in the history of the game. He stands as a model for all defensive linemen.

Jones, Parnelli (Rufus Parnell)

(1933-), race driver, was born in Texarkana, Arkansas. He quit school and began racing when he was 17. During the next 10 years, Jones became known as one of the top drivers in midget cars, sprint cars, and late-model stock cars. He competed in his first United States Auto Club (USAC) Championship race in 1959. A year later, he was named co-Rookie of the Year at the Indianapolis 500. Jones won six USAC Championship races in eight years—including the Indianapolis 500 in 1963 with a record speed of over 143 miles per hour. A versatile driver, Jones was the USAC sprint-car champion in 1961 and 1962, and the USAC stock-car champion in 1964. He estimates he won nearly 150 of the 600 races he entered before he retired at age 35. But auto racing was in his blood, and Parnelli Jones returned as a car owner and manager of a team that included such driving greats as Al Unser, Joe Leonard, and Mario Andretti.

Parnelli Jones' record proves he was one of racing's most versatile drivers. His record included major sports-car triumphs, 500-mile stock-car victories, Trans-Am sedan-racing championships, and sprint-car championships. Parnelli has also had triumphs in several off-road racing events, such as the Baja 500, the Mexican 1000, and the Mint 400. In 1963, he won the Indianapolis 500, America's greatest race.

Parnelli Jones earned important victories in almost every phase of motor racing. Following his illustrious racing career, he became the manager of a racing team.

In a stretch from 1969 through 1972, the Parnelli Jones racing team was spearheaded by Al Unser, Joe Leonard, and Mario Andretti. It became one of the most successful units in racing. The cars were designed and built at the team's shop in Torrance, California.

The team won the national championship three years running—with Unser winning the title in 1970, and Leonard taking the title in 1971 and 1972.

Rufus Parnell Jones was born on August 12, 1933, in Texarkana, Arkansas. He began his auto-racing career in 1952, competing in a stock-car event backed by the California Racing Association. In 1959, he entered his first United States Auto Club (USAC) Championship car race at Milwaukee. A year later, he shared Rookie-of-the-Year honors at Indianapolis with Bobby Marshman. Jones was the USAC sprint-car champion in 1961 and 1962.

He won the pole position at Indianapolis in both 1962 and 1963 as the fastest qualifier. In 1963, he was the first driver at Indy to qualify at over 150 miles per hour. In 1967, Jones drove the controversial four-wheel-drive STP Turbocar built by Andy Granatelli.

The car had a 260-pound tur-

Team manager Parnelli Jones (left) talks with one of his drivers, Al Unser, before the 1973 Indianapolis 500.

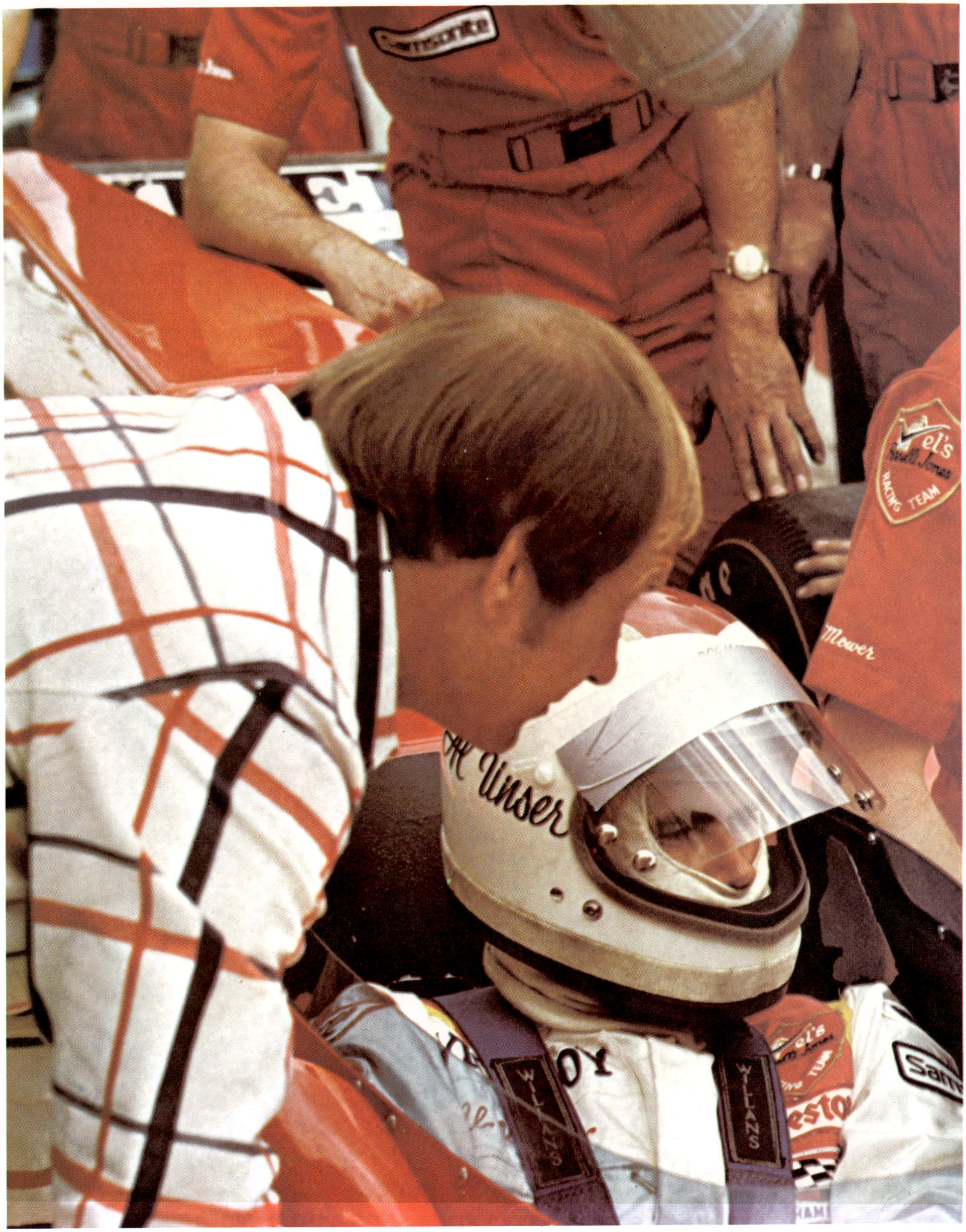
Unser
Mower
RACING TEAM
WILLANS

Jones, Parnelli

Defending champion Parnelli Jones leaps from his burning racer during an Indianapolis 500. Jones had been battling for the lead with the eventual winner, A. J. Foyt.

bine airplane engine made by Pratt and Whitney. It was designed to put out about 550 horsepower. There were few parts to wear out.

Qualified for sixth place in the starting lineup, Parnelli moved ahead on the first lap. He led for 490 miles. Then a $6 gearbox bearing failed. Parnelli was out of

Pole-sitter Parnelli, in his Agajanian Willard Battery Special, streaks past a competitor on his way to victory in the 1963 Indianapolis 500.

Crewmen pull Jones away from his burning racer after the car caught fire during a refueling stop at the 1964 Indy 500. Jones was hospitalized with burns on his arms and legs.

the race within 10 miles of victory. Because of a bad wreck, the race was stopped that year as soon as A. J. Foyt took the checkered flag. Parnelli Jones was already out. But when the race was stopped, he had run 196 laps—enough to secure 6th place. It was Jones' last trip to Indy as a driver.

By 1967, Jones had earned a good deal of money. He had come a long way from the tough neighborhood where he spent his teenage years in Torrance.

"When I was six or seven years old, my mother used to let me sit in her lap and steer our Model A Ford," Jones recalls. The car had a push-and-pull switch and could be started without a key. Parnelli's dad taught him how to drive. But he always took the distributor rotor out of the engine when he left the house so that the youngster would not be able to drive the car.

"I bought a rotor from a junkyard, and when my parents were away, I'd put it in the car and drive it in the fields," recalls Parnelli.

Parnelli Jones' high school grades were poor. He used to lie awake at night thinking about becoming a racing driver. Finally he quit school—something he was to regret in later years. Parnelli began racing jalopies in 1950 when he was 17. Ten years later, he was one of the top drivers in midget cars, sprint cars, and stock cars.

Jones, Parnelli

While leading the 1963 Indianapolis 500, Jones pits to take on fuel, tires, and a refreshing cup of water.

In 1960, Jones was a big attraction on the USAC and the National Association for Stock Car Auto Racing (NASCAR) circuits in the Middle West and the Southwest. He built a winning streak that could not be matched that year. In 1962, Jones was the only driver to win three major sprint championships.

In the space of eight years, from 1960 through 1967, Jones had one of the finest records in auto racing. His victories in Championship cars (Indy-type racers) included the Phoenix 100, the Hoosier 100, the Indianapolis 500, the Milwaukee 200, the Trenton 200, and the Milwaukee 100.

In stock-car racing, Jones won the 1963 Yankee 300 and the 1963 Pikes Peak Hill Climb. He also won five other stock-car events. He was the USAC Midwest sprint-car champion in 1960, the USAC national sprint-car champion in 1961 and 1962, and the USAC national stock-car champion in 1964.

In seven Indianapolis 500's, from 1961 through 1967, Parnelli's worst finish was 23rd in 1964. He finished in the money—among the first 10—three times, and he won the race in 1963.

Jones' worst finish came in the race that killed Eddie Sachs and Dave MacDonald. Starting in fourth position, Parnelli managed to avoid that tragic first-lap pileup. But he was forced out of the race on the

The checkered flag falls for Parnelli Jones, winner of the 47th running of the Indianapolis 500 in 1963.

54th lap when a pit fire almost cost him his life. He managed to leap out of the Agajanian-Bowes car, his driving suit in flames. He escaped with minor burns.

After the 1967 Indy 500—in which he was out after 196 laps with a faulty bearing—Parnelli planned to enter the 1968 race. But three weeks before the race, he decided to withdraw. It was a surprise to the racing world. He said he did not want to enter a race in a car that he felt could not win. He also felt that at 35 he was getting too old for high-speed competition.

After his win at Indy in 1963, Jones invested in a Torrance auto dealership owned by Vel Miletich. The two later became controlling partners in Parnelli Jones Enterprises. Jones became the president of the company. Among other things, the firm distributed tires and shock absorbers.

Jones and Miletich had put together the Viceroy and Samsoniter Special trio of Al Unser, Mario Andretti, and Joe Leonard. The Vel's-Parnelli Jones racing team became one of the more successful ones on the USAC circuit.

The great Parnelli Jones tradition is still a dominating factor in auto racing. From his days as a race-car driver to his days as manager of his own racing team, Parnelli Jones has given all that he possibly can to auto racing.

🏀 Jones, Sam (1933-),

basketball player, was born in Laurinburg, North Carolina. He played collegiate basketball at North Carolina College, a small all-black school. In 1957, Jones was chosen in the first round of the draft by the Boston Celtics of the National Basketball Association (NBA). He played guard in a reserve role behind Bob Cousy and Bill Sharman in his first few years with the Celtics. Jones found a starting berth on the team in the early 1960's, and he became the Celtics' team leader after Cousy retired following the 1962-1963 season. From the 1964-1965 campaign to the 1966-1967 season, Jones made the All-NBA second team each year—with scoring averages of 25.9, 23.2, and 22.1 in those years. He played well under the pressure of the NBA playoffs and scored the winning basket in the final game of the championship in 1962. He played on 10 championship Celtic teams during his 12-year career. After his retirement in 1969, Sam Jones served as a head coach in the collegiate ranks.

Sam Jones—like John Havlicek, K. C. Jones, and a few other Boston Celtics—had to wait his turn for stardom. Such was the tradition of Red Auerbach's Celtics of the 1950's and early 1960's. The featured stars were Bob Cousy, Bill Sharman, Tommy Heinsohn, and Frank Ramsey. These men were only replaced when they retired. Sam Jones had to wait on the bench before he could show his stuff. But once given the chance, he fit right in with the Celtics' tradition of greatness.

Sam Jones was born June 24, 1933, in Laurinburg, North Carolina, and went to North Carolina College. He became a slick backcourtman who relied on savvy and finesse rather than flair. Jones stood 6 feet, 4 inches tall and weighed 205 pounds.

North Carolina College (now North Carolina Central University) in Durham was a little-known school in 1957. But Jones was not overlooked by the eagle eye of Red Auerbach. Auerbach built the Celtics' great teams around players that other scouts had missed. So, on April 17, 1957, Jones received the first big surprise of his basketball life. The Boston Celtics made him their number-one draft pick in the annual lottery of college talent. Jones was elated at being selected number one, but he had mixed feelings about playing with the Celtics. It was great to be picked by the world champions. Yet his chances to play would have been far better had a weaker team chosen him.

Auerbach taught Sam determination and drive. They were qualities that paid off when Bob Cousy retired in 1963. Auerbach also later

A tight defense is no problem for Sam Jones as he drives by New York Knick Bill Bradley.

60

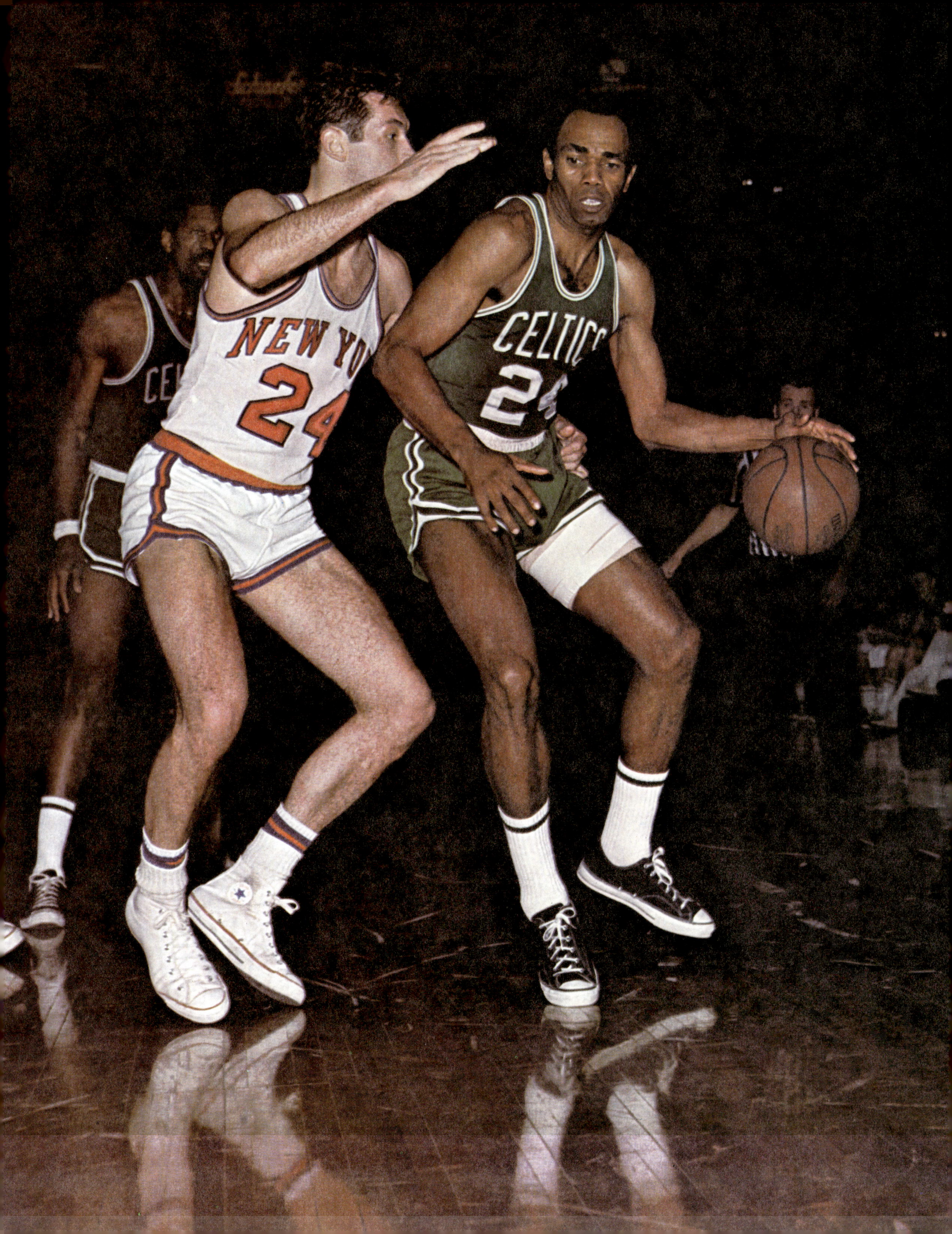
NEW YO
24
CELTICS
24

Jones, Sam

admitted that his attention was drawn to Jones by "Bones" McKinney, the famous coach at Wake Forest College in North Carolina. McKinney labeled Sam as "the best collegiate player in the entire South in 1957."

The first few years—as Sam had suspected—proved to be slow for a new player amid all that Celtic talent.

In Sam's first pro season, he saw little action, playing only 594 minutes in 56 games and averaging only 4.6 points per game. But in his second season, he began to show a trait that lasted the rest of his 12-year National Basketball Association (NBA) career. That was his great play in crucial situations. He demonstrated it in a game with the St. Louis Hawks on February 6, 1959.

Bob Cousy was sidelined by illness, and Auerbach turned to Jones to fill in. The Celtics and Hawks were leading the Eastern and Western divisions, respectively. As the game began, Sam stole the ball at the opening whistle. Throughout the game, Jones intercepted passes as well as Cousy ever had. He fed the ball to his teammates like a veteran and scored 23 points. Jones even held Cousy's old Hawk rival, Slater Martin, to eight points as the Celtics breezed to a 122-95 victory. That was the start of Sam Jones as a guard to be reckoned with in the NBA.

Playing the final game of his career, Sam Jones drives down the middle past Laker Elgin Baylor in the 1969 NBA playoffs.

Even two Los Angeles Lakers cannot stop Jones as he drives in for two points.

Jones averaged 10.7 points per game in the 1958-1959 season and raised his totals each year. Yet he was still spending time on the bench. In 1959-1960, he averaged 11.9. He raised that to 14.8 in 1960-1961. But Jones was gaining valuable experience in the playoffs.

In the last game of the 1960-1961 season, Sam was playing once again in place of the ill Cousy. Jones contributed 44 points and 13 rebounds as the Celtics nipped the Syracuse Nats, 136-134, in overtime.

In the 1961-1962 season, Sam Jones made his first really important contribution to the Celtics in the playoffs. The Celtics had breezed to the Eastern crown by 11 games and reached the final playoff series with the Los Angeles Lakers. It looked as if they might finally be taken as the Lakers dragged the series to the full seven games.

But in the final game—with two seconds left—Jones scored the deciding basket. That basket gave the Celtics their fourth straight championship and the fifth in six years.

Sam Jones increased his point-production to an average of 19.7 per game by the 1962-1963 season, aided by his patented bank shot. With Cousy gone the following year, Jones really came into his own as an NBA All-Star.

In 1964-1965, he was fully established as the go-man of the Celtics backcourt. Sam averaged 25.9 points per game—by far his best ever—even though his 19.7 in 1962-1963 had led the club. It was also the third straight year Sam Jones had led the team in shooting percentage—another trademark he was to become famous for. Jones

Jones dropped in his 10,000th career point in 1965. He receives the game ball from Celtics' coach Red Auerbach (center) and captain Bill Russell.

Jones, Sam

seldom missed the "big" shot when he was called on to take it.

During his final season with the Celtics (1968-1969), Jones looked back on his career and stated that he had worked hard for the Celtics and "was glad of it."

"Coach Auerbach had to handle 12 different personalities," Jones said, "and no one did it better. He was a dictator but what he said went and there was no dissension. [Bill] Russell had the same type of dedication."

With his arms around daughter Phyllis (left) and wife Gladys, Sam receives a standing ovation from the fans at Boston Garden. The event took place in 1969 when Jones retired after 12 years of NBA service.

So did Sam Jones, who later coached on the college level after leaving the Celtics. He coached at Federal City College in Washington, D.C., and at his alma mater, North Carolina Central University. For his contributions to basketball and athletics, Jones was the first black selected to the North Carolina Hall of Fame.

In 1970, Sam Jones stands beside his Celtic playing number (24) while waving to the crowd at Boston Garden. His number was on a banner containing the numerals of other great Boston players of the past.

In 12 years with the Celtics, Jones had a part in 10 championships. On March 28, 1967, in a playoff game against the New York Knicks, Jones set the Celtics' all-time one-game scoring record in post-season play with 51 points. In that game, he also set records for points in one half (29) and points in one quarter (19).

One of Sam Jones' greatest deeds was done off the court. One day, while out for exercise, Jones found himself playing head-to-head with a schoolyard hotshot in the city of Boston. The kid's name was Jimmy Walker. Getting to know him better through the playground games, Jones found out that this brilliant young player was unable to attend college. So Sam dug into his pockets and shelled out $1200 so that Jimmy Walker could go to college. Walker later established himself as an All-American at Providence College in Rhode Island and later as a standout in the NBA.

Sam Jones was that kind of guy. "I feel I've had a wonderful 12 years with the Celtics," he said at his retirement. "After being on 10 championship teams, I feel sorry for those guys who never got the chance."

Sam Jones was not just part of those championship teams. He was—as the record books show—the man who made many of them possible.

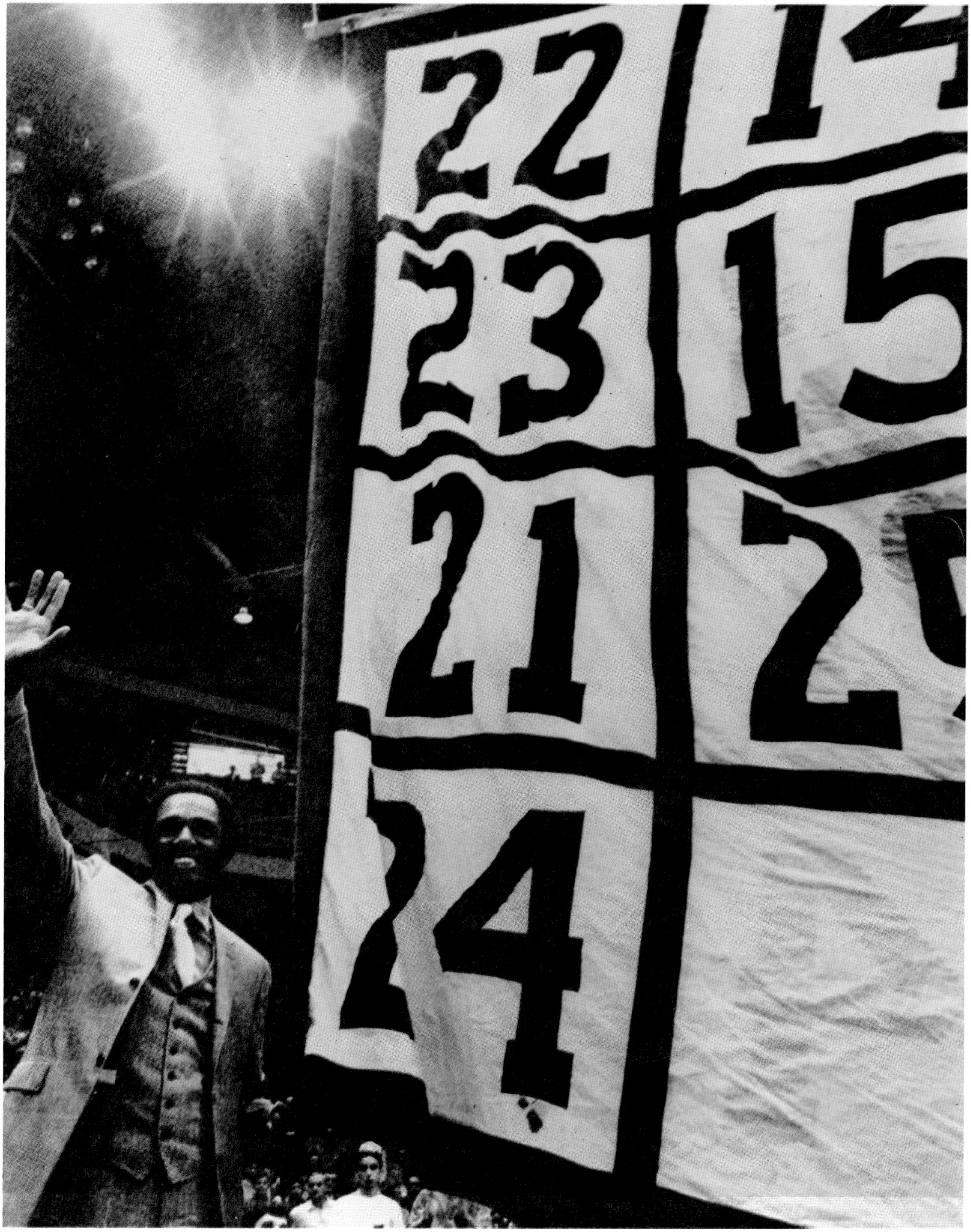
22
23
21
24
15

Joyce, Joan

(1940-   ), softball player, basketball player, and golfer, was born in Waterbury, Connecticut. At 13, she began competing in fast-pitch softball leagues. Joan later earned All-America honors in basketball. During her softball career, she played for the Stratford (Connecticut) Reybestos Brakettes, the Orange (California) Lionettes, and the Connecticut Falcons, a professional team. She led her teams to 19 national championships and four professional titles. As a pitcher, Joyce compiled a 658-46 record, including 139 no-hitters and 41 perfect games. Her fast ball was clocked at 116 miles per hour. Baseball greats Ted Williams and Henry Aaron were among her victims at the plate. A marvelous all-round athlete, Joan Joyce made the Ladies Professional Golf Association (LPGA) tour in 1977.

When books are written about the sports history of the United States, they will indicate that the women's movement in competitive athletics began in the 1970's. At that time, women began getting the opportunities and recognition long accorded men.

Joan Joyce's movement in American sports began about two decades too soon. Her basketball stardom was confined to the 1960's, before women got much recognition on the courts. Joan's heroics in her best sport—fast-pitch softball—came before the women's sports boom of the mid-1970's. And unfortunately, her golf career started when she was past her athletic prime. Regardless, she is considered the finest all-round woman athlete since Babe Didrikson Zaharias.

Joan Mary Joyce was born on August 18, 1940, in Waterbury, Connecticut. Her interest in sports was encouraged by her father. He used to take her to the playground while babysitting for Joan and her brother. As a youngster, she participated in many sports.

Joan was particularly gifted in softball. At 13, she began playing in top-flight competition. Joan was a pitcher for the Stratford (Connecticut) Raybestos Brakettes for 18 years, the Orange (California) Lionettes for three seasons, and the professional Connecticut Falcons for four years. Her teams captured a total of 19 national championships. The professional Falcons, of which Joyce was part owner, won the women's professional title all four years Joan played in the league.

Her individual statistics were even more amazing than the teams for which she played. During her pitching career, she won 658 games—far more than any major-league baseball pitcher. She lost only 46 games. Eight of those losses came in 1979, when Joan, at age 39, was trying to combine softball with a professional golf career.

Of her 658 victories, 139 were no-hitters and 41 were perfect games. She wound up her amateur career in 1975, with a streak of 229

Joyce led the Connecticut Falcons to four professional championships in as many years.

scoreless innings and 52 consecutive victories.

Over the years, Joyce pitched about a third of her team's games. When she was not on the mound, the 5-foot, 10-inch, 160-pound athlete played in the field. Her career batting average was close to .325.

Should anyone scoff at the competition in which Joyce built up such marvelous statistics, that person would be advised not to talk to baseball Hall-of-Famers Ted Williams and Hank Aaron. They are among Joan's many victims. In fact, she may be the only pitcher to ever strike out both men. Joan, whose pitch has been clocked at 116 miles an hour, completely baffled the baseball greats.

Joyce pitched against Williams in 1962, the year after he retired from baseball. "He came to Waterbury," she recalled, "and I was throwing stuff that he had never seen. There were 10,000 people there, and I shouldn't have done it, even though he told me to pitch all-out. I felt bad because Ted is a friend of mine."

Joyce tantalized Williams at the plate for about 10 minutes. He watched fast ball after fast ball come his way—about 30 pitches in all.

Joan's fast ball was clocked at 116 miles per hour.

The best he could do was to foul off a couple pitches.

Aaron, baseball's all-time home-run hitter, was even more frustrated in his appearance against Joyce. The confrontation occurred during a 1978 game. The Falcons played a team called Con's Kings, for whom Aaron was a guest performer. Henry could not get his bat on any of her six pitches.

Joan has stated, more than once, that her goal in sports is not to prove herself against men. "I can go out now and play against them, and I have," she remarked in 1979.

Joyce, Joan

During her amazing softball career, Joan Joyce threw 139 no-hitters and 41 perfect games.

Joyce whiffs baseball great Henry Aaron in a 1978 charity exhibition.

Joan fires a drop curve during a game in China. She toured the country with the Connecticut Falcons in 1979.

Although known for her pitching exploits, Joyce was also a fine hitter.

"But I don't see that as a big deal—or a goal. I don't want to take a chance getting hurt while trying to prove that. I know, as an athlete, I compete as hard and with the same desire as men."

It is that competitive desire that made Joan a basketball champion earlier in her career. In 1961, she led all scorers in an Amateur Athletic Union (AAU) women's tournament. She earned AAU All-America honors in 1961, 1962, 1965, and 1967. Joyce averaged 25 points a game during her basketball career.

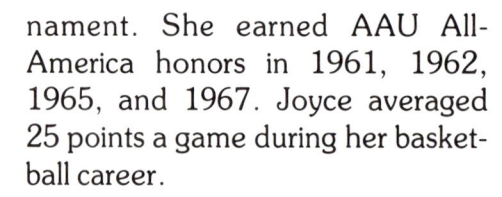

With the same competitive zeal, Joan began concentrating on golf in the late 1970's. She joined the Ladies Professional Golf Association (LPGA) in 1977. She was at a disadvantage because she had not played as a youth. Still, she became one of the longest hitters on the tour, booming drives as far as 260 yards.

Joan Joyce never gained the national limelight. She did, however, help pioneer the women's sports movement in America.

Joyce lines up a putt during an LPGA tournament in 1977.

Joan Joyce and Billie Jean King announce the creation of the Connecticut Falcons in 1976.

⏱ Juantorena, Alberto

AHL-*BARE*-TOH WAHN-TOH-*RAY*-NAH (1951-   ), middle-distance runner, was born in Santiago de Cuba, Cuba. Alberto worked in the sugar cane fields as a youngster and played basketball in his spare time. He began running track in 1971 because his basketball career was not as promising as he had hoped. His specialty became the 400-meter dash. At the 1972 Olympics in Munich, West Germany, he made it to the semifinals of the 400-meter run before being disqualified. He went on to rank third in the world in 1973 and first in 1974. An injury in 1975 kept him out of competition until late in the year. Juantorena then began running 800 meters as well as the 400. He entered both events at the 1976 Olympics in Montreal, Canada, and won both. No other Olympian had ever accomplished the feat. Juantorena was so good in the 800 meters that he set a world record of 1 minute, 43.5 seconds. When the year was over, he was undefeated in both events. Alberto Juantorena was named Athlete of the Year by the *Track & Field News.*

The 400-meter run is the longest dash event. It requires a competitor to go all-out for a quarter of a mile. The 800-meter run is the shortest of the distance events, requiring a sense of pace for about a half-mile.

A 6-foot, 2-inch, 185-pound Cuban galloped to victory in both events at the 1976 Olympic Games in Montreal, Quebec, Canada. The feat had never been accomplished in Olympic history. The runner's name was Alberto Juantorena, and his nickname was *El Caballo,* which means "The Horse" in Spanish. His combined strength and sense of pace had never before been seen in one runner.

Born December 3, 1951, in Santiago de Cuba, Cuba, Alberto worked in the sugar cane fields as a youth. He became a fine basketball player, and eventually, he was good enough to make Cuba's national team. But Alberto turned to track when he was 20. He could see his basketball career was going nowhere.

In 1971, Juantorena ran his first 400-meter race. He clocked a surprising time of 51 seconds in tennis shoes. By the next year, he was on Cuba's Olympic team and heading for the Games at Munich, West Germany.

At Montreal in 1976, Alberto Juantorena of Cuba became the first man in Olympic history to win the 400-meter and 800-meter races. Here, he receives his gold medal and congratulations after capturing the 800.

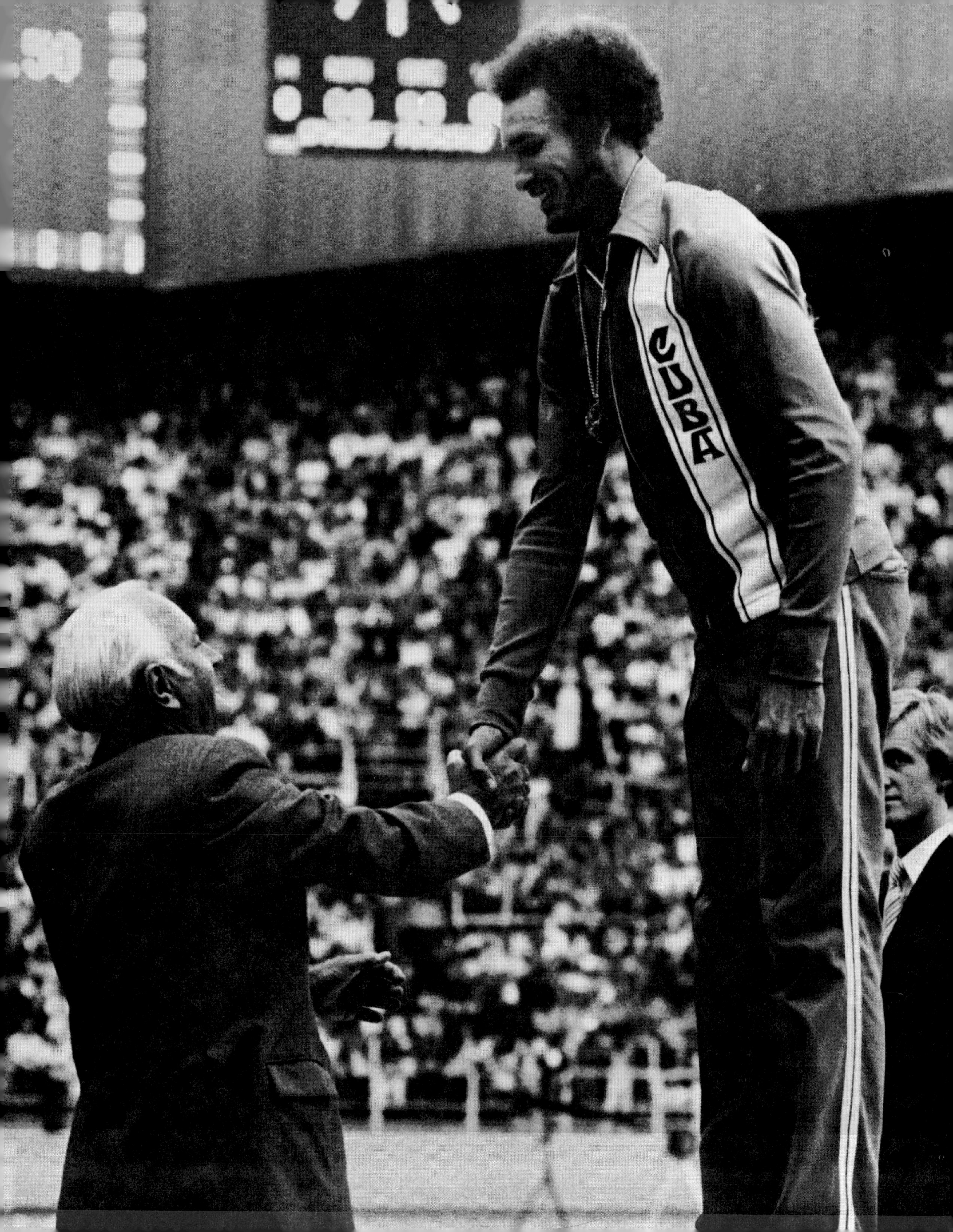
CUBA

Juantorena, Alberto

Coached by a Polish trainer named Zygmunt Zabierzowski, Alberto ran against the world's best 400-meter men at Munich and held his own. He clocked times below 46 seconds. He got as far as the semifinals before bowing out. The track world foresaw a great future for him.

Juantorena returned to Cuba and studied at the University of Havana. And he continued to surprise the track world. In 1973, he ranked third in the world for the 400 meters.

His coach, Zabierzowski, admitted, "Munich was too early for us. We had too much to learn, too much to refine."

The learning took place in 1973. The victories came in 1974. Alberto went undefeated in the 400, and his best time was 44.7 seconds. At the end of the year, he was ranked number one in the world.

In 1975, Alberto was hampered by a serious foot injury. A magazine photo showed him with his leg in a cast after surgery. Outside of Cuba, many wondered how serious his injury was. Juantorena showed them later that year. He finished second in the 400-meter run at the Pan-American Games.

As Alberto trained for the Olympics in 1976, it was clear that he was one of the men to beat in the 400. He was undefeated in 1976 before the Montreal Games. But suddenly, he had also become a good 800-meter man—much to everyone's surprise. Juantorena had run the 800 to make himself stronger for the 400. But he found out he was good in that event, too. He was timed at 1 minute, 46.1 seconds in a national meet and 1 minute, 45.2 seconds in Italy. The world record was 1 minute, 43.7 seconds.

Juantorena tried to dismiss the thought of doubling in the 400 and 800 meters at Montreal. "The 800 will have to wait until next year," he said. "I wish to be the Olympic 400 champion first."

Then Alberto ran a 1-minute, 44.9-second 800 two weeks before the Olympics. He decided to give the 800 a try, though he had only run the event a half-dozen times.

It would not be easy. No man had ever achieved a double win in the 400 and 800 meters. With both fields filled by outstanding American runners in 1976, Juantorena was not even sure of winning one gold medal.

Another problem was that the 800-meter run came first. There was the threat that *El Caballo* might not be strong enough to handle both races. (In the Olympics, runners must run three preliminaries before making the final of the 400 and two before the final of the 800.) Juantorena also had the additional chore of running for his nation's 1600-meter relay team.

On July 23, he began his task. That day, he won an 800-meter heat. The next day, he won a semifinal heat with a time of 1 minute, 45.9 seconds.

July 25 marked the anniversary date of Cuba's revolution. Juantorena, beaming with confidence, lined up for the 800-meter final. He went out fast, got the lead at about 200 meters, and continued to press on. He was sprinting at the finish like a 400-meter man. Alberto won with a time of 1 minute, 43.5 seconds—a world record.

Cuba now had its first gold medal ever in track and field. Some people said Juantorena celebrated the Cuban revolution with one of his own—he had revolutionized the 800 into a sprinter's race.

The following day, Alberto played it safe in the 400. He finished third in his heat and second in his quarter-final. After a day of rest, Juantorena opened up and won the semifinals.

Alberto Juantorena was ready for the 400-meter finals on July 29. The Americans were also ready with three outstanding runners. One of them, Fred Newhouse, said, "I think we can run him [Alberto] right out of a medal."

Newhouse tried. He had a three-yard lead over Juantorena

Juantorena crosses the finish line in the 400-meter run and looks back at second-place-finisher Fred Newhouse of the U.S. Alberto's Olympic time was 44.26 seconds—the fastest clocking ever at sea level.

halfway through the race. Another American, Herman Frazier, stayed in front of the Cuban, too. But in the stretch, it was *El Caballo*. He sped past the Americans to finish with a time of 44.26 seconds. It was the third fastest 400 ever run and the fastest in history at sea level.

At 24, Juantorena had completed a dream double. For the rest of the year he stayed undefeated in both events.

For his efforts, *Track & Field News* magazine named him Athlete of the Year for 1976. In a poll of United Press International (UPI) European sports editors, Alberto Juantorena was named Sportsman of the Year.

Jurgensen, Sonny

(Christian Adolph) (1934-   ), football player, was born in Wilmington, North Carolina. In high school, he was an all-round athlete. He played football, baseball, and basketball. As Duke University's quarterback, Jurgensen did not pass much, but he played well enough to be drafted in the fourth round by the Philadelphia Eagles of the National Football League (NFL). In his first full season as a starting quarterback in 1961, Jurgensen set the NFL record for pass completions (235) and passing yardage (3723), while tying the record for touchdown passes at that time (32). In 1964, he was traded to the Washington Redskins. He became one of the greatest quarterbacks of all time, although he never played on a great team in his prime. Leading the NFL in passing in 1967 and 1969, he set league records in 1967 by throwing 508 passes and completing 288. In his 18-year career, Jurgensen completed 57.1 per cent of his passes for 32,224 yards. He also tossed 255 touchdown passes. After being plagued by injuries, Jurgensen retired after the 1974 season and became a sports announcer.

Many football experts regard Sonny Jurgensen as the finest passer in the history of the game. But during his career, he was held back by serious injuries and by lack of support from his teammates.

Jurgensen could get rid of the ball faster than almost any other quarterback. This allowed him to wait longer to pick out receivers. He is said to have had the quickest wrist in pro football. He could also weave like a boxer and then throw while off-balance. There were few better pocket passers or quarterbacks more skilled at beating the rush.

Jurgensen was a natural athlete and a fierce competitor. He was always his team's top performer in all the sports he tried. He was also the team comedian and its fastest talker.

Christian Adolph "Sonny" Jurgensen, III, was born August 23, 1934, in Wilmington, North Carolina. At New Hanover High School in Wilmington, he became an all-round athlete. He starred in football, baseball, and basketball. Hanover High was the same school that NFL quarterback Roman Gabriel later attended.

At Duke University, Sonny Jurgensen played football, but he did little passing. Ace Parker, former Brooklyn Dodger star, was on the staff at Duke. Parker strongly recommended Jurgensen to the pros. Jurgensen was then drafted in

Spotting a hole in the defense, Jurgensen changes the play at the line of scrimmage.

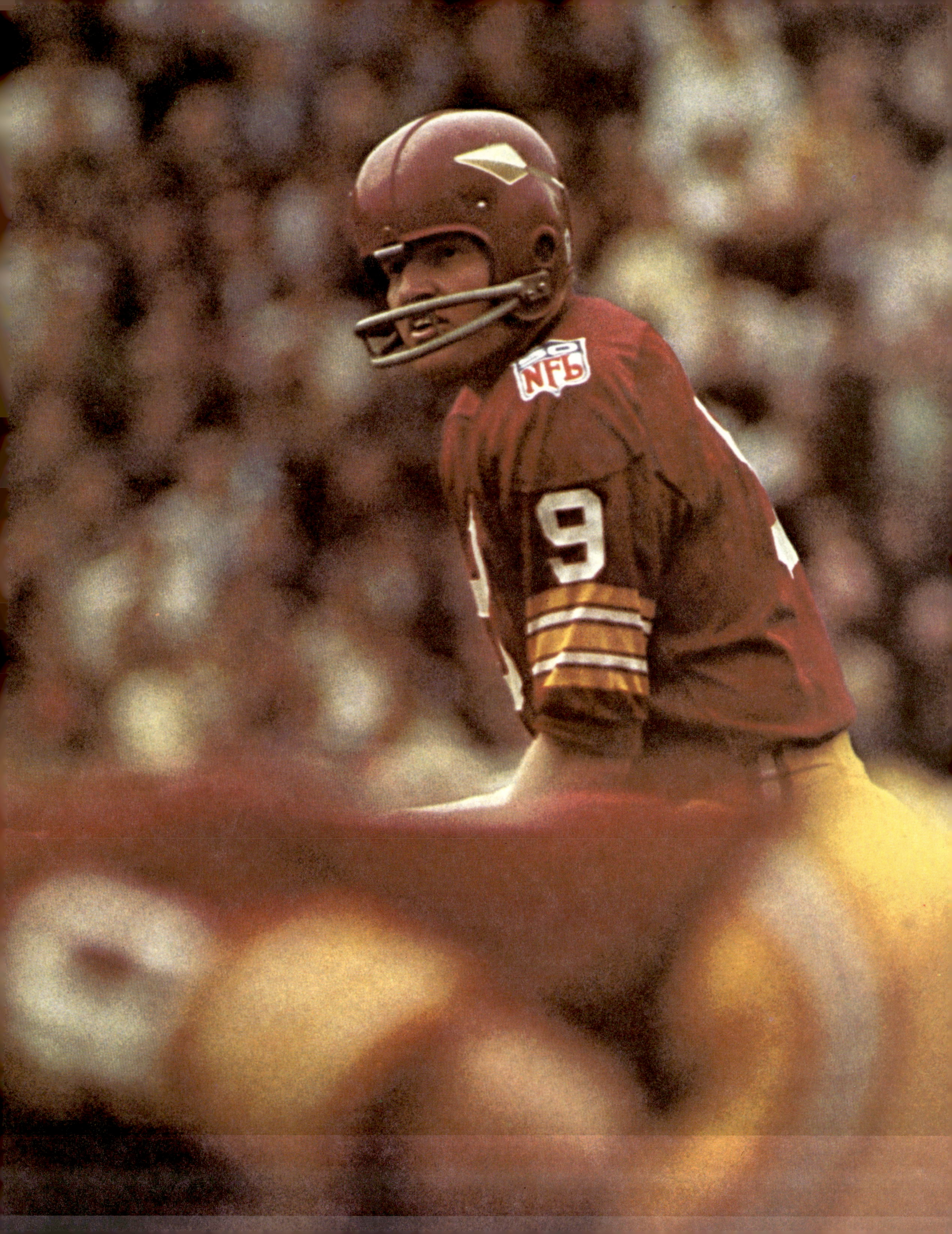
NFL
9

Jurgensen, Sonny

The 1970 exhibition season got started when Jurgensen passed the Washington Redskins to a 45-21 victory over the Boston Patriots. Jurgensen heaved four TD passes that afternoon.

Jurgensen strains every muscle to make this throw.

Jurgensen was a standout during his college days at Duke University.

the fourth round by the Philadelphia Eagles of the National Football League (NFL).

In his rookie season at Philadelphia in 1957, Sonny worked with Bobby Thomason, a sidearm thrower, then playing his last year. After the Eagles lost their first three games, Jurgensen was made the starting quarterback against the Cleveland Browns. He led the Eagles to a 17-7 upset. He was the key player in three of the Eagles' four victories that season. As a rookie, he threw 70 passes.

Star quarterback Norm Van Brocklin was brought to Philadelphia the next year, and Jurgensen was forced into the background. In 1958 he tossed 22 passes, in 1959 he threw only five, and in 1960 he threw 44. But Sonny Jurgensen admits he learned much from Van Brocklin. "Particularly, he taught me how to hold off tacklers with fake throws," he said. Jurgensen kept his light-hearted attitude during those years on the bench. He went into the game only to hold the ball for the placekicker. He called himself "the best-paid ball-handler in the league." Van Brocklin retired after the Eagles won the NFL championship during the 1960 season, and Jurgensen at last got his chance to lead the team.

In 1961, his first season as a starter, he broke the NFL record for pass completions (235), set a pass

Jurgensen takes a quick look at the defense before calling signals.

In the 1969 season, Sonny Jurgensen led the NFL in passing yardage with 3102.

yardage mark of 3723 yards, and tied the record of 32 touchdown passes in a single season. In a game against the Washington Redskins, the Eagles gained only 12 yards rushing. But Jurgensen passed for 436 yards. Sonny took the Eagles to seven victories in their first eight games. Two defeats by the New York Giants caused them to miss the Eastern title by half a game.

Jurgensen suffered a dislocated shoulder in the Playoff Bowl. The bad shoulder affected his passing the next season, and 26 of his passes were intercepted. The Eagles fell to last place after their four main receivers were injured.

In 1963, Jurgensen walked out of camp because he thought the Eagles did not appreciate his talent. He took with him the number-two quarterback, King Hill. The short strike won Jurgensen a $30,000 contract, and it got $20,000 for Hill, even though he hardly ever played.

In 1964, the Eagles traded Jurgensen and Jimmy Carr, a defensive back, to Washington for Norm Snead and Claude Crabb. With the Washington Redskins, Jurgensen began a seven-year streak of great passing. In those seven years he passed for 2934, 2367, 3209, 3747, 1980, 3102, and 2354 yards before he was injured in 1971. He won the NFL

Jurgensen, Sonny

Jurgensen lofts a pass high over the Pittsburgh Steelers.

passing title in 1967 for the first time, after ranking second to Bart Starr in 1966. In 1967, Jurgensen set NFL records for the most passes thrown, most passes completed, and most yards gained. He led in touchdown passes thrown and had the lowest percentage of interceptions. Jurgensen also set the mark for the highest number of 400-yard passing games in NFL history. He accomplished the remarkable feat five times during his career.

Sonny Jurgensen had been fighting elbow trouble for several seasons. In May 1968, he had calcium deposits removed from his throwing elbow. The operation cut down both his play and his accuracy. To play, he had to be taped up like a mummy.

After his elbow operation, Sonny did not play in the 1968 season until the final pre-season game. Then, his passing gave the Redskins a win over Pittsburgh. After the fifth game, he was hit by another injury—fractured ribs. But he kept on playing. Then he caught a severe case of flu.

But in 1969 he was back, winning his second NFL passing title. Jurgensen had 274 completions in 442 attempts. The completion mark was topped only by Jurgensen's own record of 288 set in 1967. He became the only passer ever to gain more than 3000 yards in a season five times.

Sonny Jurgensen had one of his passes intercepted by the Miami Dolphins during the 1971 exhibition season and tried to make the tackle. This is the result. Jurgensen had to have corrective surgery.

Jurgensen made the All-NFL teams in 1961, 1964, 1966, and 1969. He played in the 1966 Pro Bowl game but had to pass it up five times because of injuries.

Jurgensen was such a successful passer because he could throw well even when off-balance. "Some quarterbacks have to go back and set up and stay there," he explained. "I have control even from the weirdest positions. I slide around a lot from side to side, because the defensive linemen have become so tall that I can't get the ball over them sometimes. I've got to find a clear path for throwing."

In spite of all his brilliant pass plays, Jurgensen was not a successful team leader. It was Bill Kilmer who awakened the Washington Redskins in 1971. Kilmer led the team to the Super Bowl in the 1972 season, even though his passing talent did not compare to Sonny Jurgensen's.

In 1974, the shoulder and elbow injuries that plagued Jurgensen throughout his career finally caught up with him. He retired with his place among the top quarterbacks in the game assured.

During the winter of 1968, Sonny had an operation on his throwing arm. To make sure that nothing went wrong, Sonny soaked his arm in ice water for 10 minutes after each practice session in training camp.

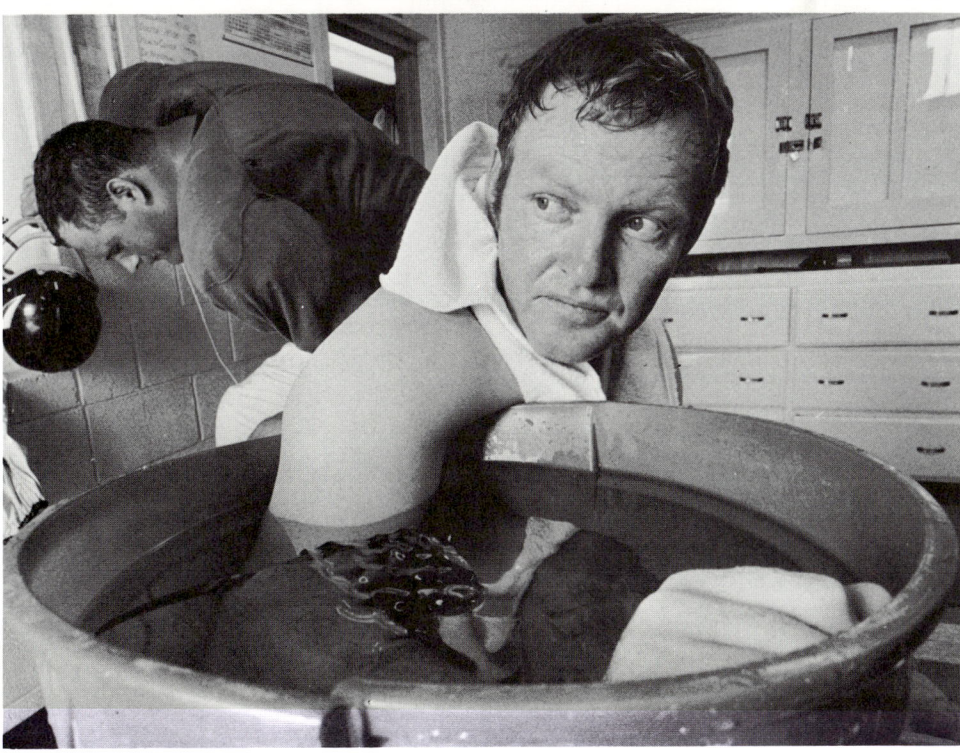

Kahanamoku, Duke

KUH-*HAHN*-UH-*MOH*-KOO (1890-1968), swimmer, surfer, and water polo player, was born in Honolulu, Hawaii. He became interested in surfing and helped bring popularity to the sport. Arriving in California in 1912, Kahanamoku used the "crawl," still unpopular with American swimmers. He dominated freestyle sprint races from 1912 until 1924. He won gold medals in the 100-meter freestyle in the Olympic Games of 1912 and 1920. He also won a gold medal for the United States in the 800-meter freestyle relay at the 1920 Olympics, and two silver medals. Establishing record times in the 100-meter and 100-yard freestyle events, Kahanamoku won the U.S. national outdoor title at 100 yards in 1916, 1917, and 1920, and the indoor event in 1912. He then pursued an acting career in the late 1920's. Kahanamoku later became an excellent water polo player, making the U.S. Olympic water polo team in 1932. In 1965, Kahanamoku was elected to the International Swimming Hall of Fame.

Surfer, lifeguard, actor, public official, teacher, water polo player, and Olympic champion swimmer—these were just some of the titles Duke Kahanamoku earned. He is remembered best for his three Olympic gold medals and two Olympic silver medals in swimming, and for his active role in making surfing popular.

Duke Paoa Kahanamoku was born August 14, 1890, in Honolulu, Hawaii. He was the oldest of six boys. He was named after his father, who was born during the Duke of Edinburgh's visit to Hawaii in July 1869. The boy grew up bearing his name proudly. He excelled in everything he tried.

Most of Duke's childhood was spent on the white sands of Waikiki Beach. He ran, jumped, swam, climbed trees, and played in the surf at every chance. He grew to be a tall and strong young man.

Duke became devoted to surfing. He watched the older boys struggle with their boards in the fast Hawaiian surf. Duke saw that all of the boys used short surfboards of heavy redwood, and few had much success in the sport. While he was still in his teens, Duke switched to the longer boards used by his royal Hawaiian ancestors. Soon everybody changed to longer boards, because they made surfing easier. The sport began to gain in popularity. Duke and his brother Sammy became the best surfers at Waikiki Beach.

Duke's success in surfing carried over into swimming. Duke was over 6 feet tall and had very strong arms and legs, developed by count-

Duke Kahanamoku was a member of every U.S. Olympic swimming team from 1912 to 1928.

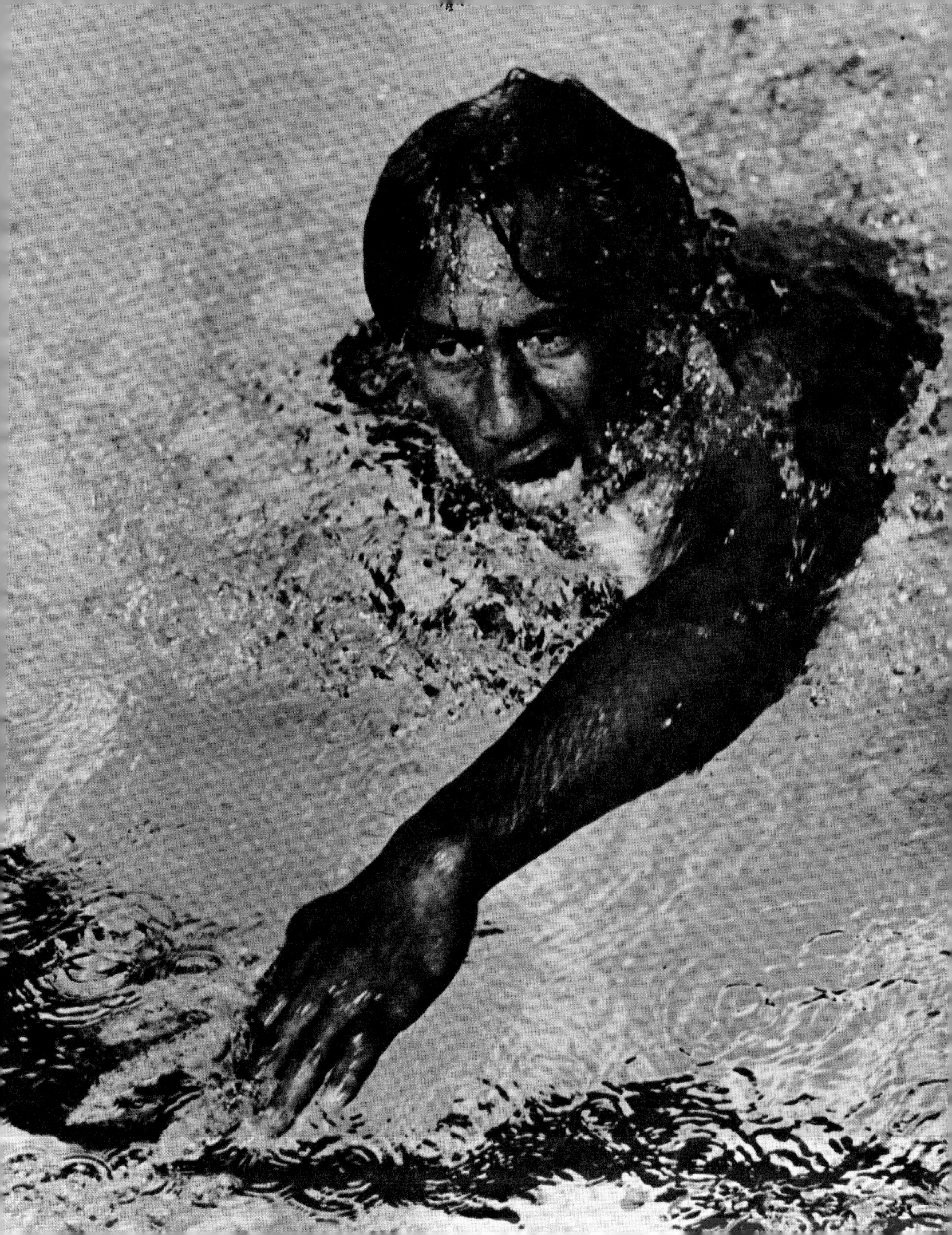

Kahanamoku, Duke

Always in love with his native Hawaii, Duke served as official greeter for the city of Honolulu.

One of the world's all-time great athletes, Duke proudly displays some of the hundreds of trophies he won.

less hours of swimming and paddling his surfboard out to the waves. To go fast enough to catch rides on the waves, Duke swam the "crawl" stroke, used for generations by the people of the South Pacific. Although he was not the first to use the crawl in international competition, it was his successes that made the stroke so popular around the world.

His strength and form kept Duke supreme in freestyle racing from 1912 until 1924. At 21, Duke left the Hawaiian Islands to compete on the mainland. He won the 1912 U.S. national indoor 100-yard freestyle championship. He then easily won the gold medal in the 1912 Olympic Games in Stockholm, Sweden. In the Olympic semifinals, Duke had equaled the world record for the 100 meters with a time of 1 minute, 2.4 seconds (1:02.4).

Duke hoped to compete in the next Olympics, to be held in Germany in 1916. Meanwhile he set a new world record for the 100 meters on a straight course. He then set his sights on the 100-yard freestyle mark. In 1913, he posted 54.5, breaking the record for the 100-yard event. In his travels to different swimming meets, Duke took time out to meet people on the beaches. He showed them his great skill with the surfboard, and soon the sport became widely popular.

When World War I began, the hope of holding the 1916 Olympic Games vanished. But Duke refused to let up in his training and in his quest for improvement. He smashed the 100-yard mark again when he won his first U.S. outdoor national championship in 1916. He won the 100-yard event again in 1917 and 1920.

In 1920, the Olympic Games were held in Antwerp, Belgium. It was the chance Duke Kahanamoku had been waiting for. The 100-meter event was held on August 14, the opening day of the Games and also Duke's birthday. Duke easily made it to the finals. He then faced the task of beating his Hawaiian teammate, Pua Kealoha. Duke exploded at the start and stroked out to a long lead. His first-place time of 1:00.4 broke both the world record and the Olympic record. Before Duke could count the win as his own, one of the swimmers claimed he had been crowded during the race. Since no lane lines separated the swimmers, they often came close or collided. The judges ordered the race repeated. Duke won again—with a time that was one whole second faster than his time in the 1912 Olympics. Duke also swam in the 800-meter freestyle relay, helping the U.S. team to a gold medal.

Duke Kahanamoku returned

Kahanamoku was always willing to help young swimmers.

to the Olympics in 1924, in Paris. He won a silver medal for second place in the 100-meter freestyle event. The gold medal was won by Johnny Weissmuller in Olympic-record time. Duke's brother Sammy finished third for the bronze medal. The U.S. took a clean sweep of the 100-meter freestyle.

In 1925, Duke again went to California. There, he became the lifeguard captain at the Santa Monica Beach Club. One evening Duke and his friends camped out on Corona Del Mar Beach. Early in the morning a huge storm swell upset a large fishing boat full of men. Duke and his friends swam out into the huge waves and saved 12 of the fishermen. Duke paddled out on his surfboard and saved eight, bringing them back to shore one at a time.

Duke Kahanamoku's rescue effort won him fame. It even helped him become an actor.

When Duke took up water polo, he was good enough to make the team for the 1932 Olympic Games in Los Angeles.

But the lure of home and Waikiki Beach was too much. Duke returned to Hawaii. He continued surfing, and he built a surfboard 16 feet long, weighing 126 pounds. Few men besides Duke were strong enough to carry it to the ocean and paddle it out to the huge waves.

Duke loved Hawaii. He served nine terms as sheriff of Honolulu. He also served as Ambassador-at-Large for Hawaii and official greeter for Honolulu. He was elected to the International Swimming Hall of Fame in 1965.

Those who best remember Duke Kahanamoku recall far more than his many awards and titles. They talk about the smiling, handsome man who made friends around the globe.

Kaline, Al KAY-LINE (1934-),

baseball player, was born in Baltimore, Maryland. As a 15-year-old sandlot star, he was spotted by a Detroit scout. Three years later, Kaline signed a $35,000 bonus with Detroit and went directly to the major leagues—a jump few players have ever made. At 20, in 1955, he belted 27 home runs, drove in 102 runs, and hit .340, becoming the youngest man ever to win the American League batting title. In 1959, Kaline hit .327 with 27 homers. In 1962, he hit .304 with 29 homers and 94 runs batted in, though playing in only 100 games. In the 1968 World Series, he led the Tigers to victory over the St. Louis Cardinals. Although he was an outstanding hitter, those who saw Kaline play will probably best remember him for his remarkable defensive abilities. Before retiring in 1974, Kaline hit 399 home runs, collected 3007 hits, and earned a berth on *The Sporting News* All-Star fielding team nine times.

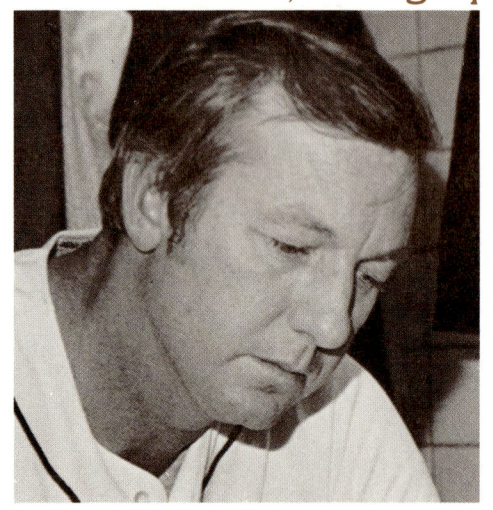

Throughout his long career with the Detroit Tigers, two trademarks characterized Al Kaline—class and consistency. The baseball superstar went about his brilliant career with a minimum of flair and a maximum of dignity. It was not surprising that after the 1972 season, Kaline was presented the Roberto Clemente Memorial Award for his distinguished service to baseball. He considered the award his greatest honor.

Kaline received many other honors during his remarkable playing career. He was the youngest man ever to win an American League batting title. He was also honored several times for his defensive skills. He was twice named the outstanding player in the American League by *The Sporting News*. And he was named to the All-Star team 15 times.

Albert William Kaline was born December 19, 1934. When he was 15, he was spotted on the sandlots of Baltimore, Maryland, by Tiger scout Ed Katalinas. Three years later, in 1953, Kaline signed a $35,000 bonus contract with the Tigers. He leaped directly from sandlot baseball into the major leagues. The following year, Kaline played a full season with the Tigers. Despite being only 19 and a year removed from sandlot ball, he batted a respectable .276.

Katalinas wrote in Al Kaline's scouting report that the young ballplayer "ran with excellent speed, had excellent body control, was a natural outfielder and was the best player I ever scouted." Katalinas began to look like a prophet. In 1955 there was no doubt.

The Tigers were more than pleased with the progress of this 6-foot, 2-inch, 184-pound young prospect. Kaline, in only 2½ years as a major-leaguer, had arrived. He won the American League batting title that year with an astonishing .340 average. He was 20—the youngest man to ever accomplish this feat. While he never won another title, he had nine .300 sea-

84

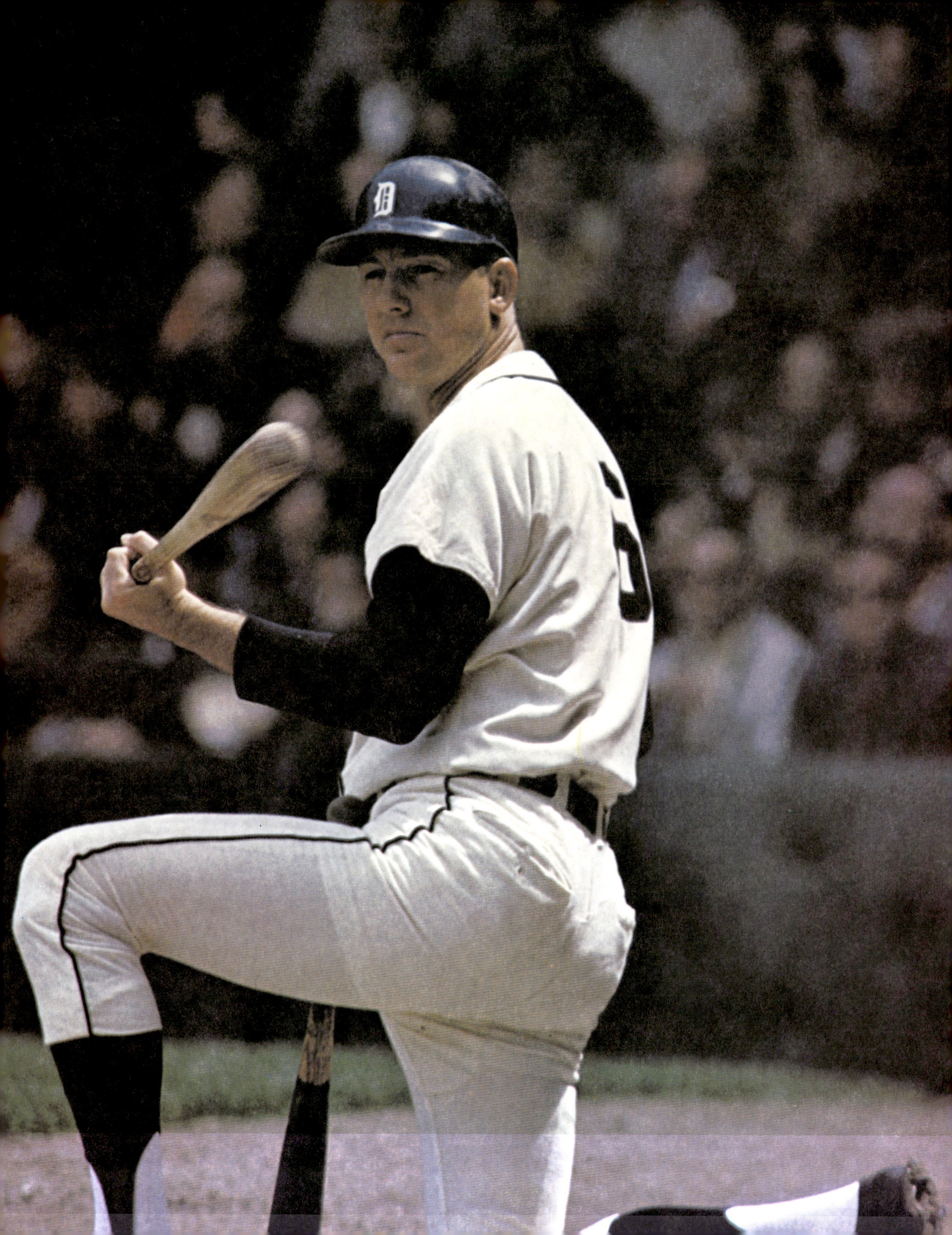

Kaline, Al

The Tigers' reliable Number 6, Al Kaline, awaits his turn at bat.

Rubbing dirt on his hands between pitches, Kaline looks to the dugout for instructions.

sons in his career. Al Kaline also led the league in total bases in 1955 with 321—the end product of 27 home runs, 24 doubles, eight triples, and 141 singles.

Curiously, that 1955 season has often been blamed by many baseball observers as Al Kaline's one major downfall. Kaline was never able to compete with his own fantastic early success. So he never really reached his potential as one of the game's all-time hitting stars. The nearest he got to the .340 batting record was .327 in 1959. But he gained respect as an all-round player and earned a place among the game's great outfielders.

Other problems barring Kaline's progress toward greatness were untimely injuries. In 1962, Kaline had made his best start in seven years. But during a Tiger-New York Yankees game, Kaline was hurt. He fractured his right collarbone while making one of his usual diving catches for a final out, helping the Tigers win, 2-0. Kaline could not return to action until late in July. But he still batted .304 with 29 homers and 94 RBI's—all in only 100 games.

In 1967, the Tigers missed out on the American League pennant by one game in a heated four-team race. Kaline had another tough break that season when he fractured his right hand. He was out for a month. Yet Kaline wound up batting .308 with 25 homers and 78 RBI's. And he was selected for the All-Star fielding team for the seventh straight year.

In 1968, the Tigers finally won a pennant. But again, injuries almost caused Kaline to miss out. On May 26, he was hit by a pitch that broke his right arm. Al Kaline

In 1968 World Series action, Kaline belts a homer against the St. Louis Cardinals. He batted .379 in the seven-game Series.

was on the disabled list for more than a month. His batting average dipped to .287 that year and his home-run production dropped off to just 10. But in the World Series, Kaline showed that he was always at his best under pressure.

One of the game's greatest clutch players, Kaline batted .379 in the Tigers' victorious Series over the St. Louis Cardinals. He also drilled a pair of home runs, drove in eight runs, and tied four post-season classic records. Included were most hits in one inning (2), most runs in one inning (2), and most putouts in one game by a right fielder (7). He was also flawless in the field for the Tigers in the Series.

In 1972, after Kaline had four straight sub-.300 seasons, many people thought he might be reaching the end of the line. But he bounced back with a .313 average, including a hot spell down the stretch that carried the Tigers into the playoffs against Oakland. Maybe it was a sign of what his whole career had been about—delivering when he was most needed.

During the American League playoffs in 1972, against the eventual world champion Oakland A's, Kaline again played outstandingly for the Tigers. He was, by that time, 38—getting old for a ballplayer. He batted only .263 but scored three runs, had eight total bases, one home run, and a run batted in. As usual, he also made several brilliant defensive plays in right field.

Kaline, Al

Baseball Commissioner Bowie Kuhn presents an award to 18-year veteran Al Kaline before a 1970 game between the Tigers and the Minnesota Twins. It was "Al Kaline Day."

Al Kaline's All-Star Game totals parallel his performance in the World Series. In 13 All-Star Game appearances, he batted .324 with two homers and six RBI's, while never committing an error. Again, under pressure conditions, Al Kaline consistently came through.

Despite his .297 lifetime batting average, Kaline will probably be remembered more for his prowess as a defensive player. Even after he reached the late stages of his career, Kaline gunned down many a runner with his famed right arm. In 1973, then-Tiger manager Bill Martin said when asked about his "old" ball club, "There isn't any manager in the league who wouldn't want Al Kaline playing right field for him—even at 39 years old." The records show a Kaline error was almost as rare as a Kaline failure in a clutch-hitting situation.

In 1974, Kaline retired after playing 22 years with the Tigers. During his career he smacked 399 home runs, collected 3007 hits, and earned nine berths on *The Sporting News* All-Star fielding team and 10 Gold Glove awards. He was truly a model of consistency. Al Kaline was inducted into the Baseball Hall of Fame in 1980.

In a 1957 game at Yankee Stadium, Kaline leaps into the stands in a vain attempt to catch a line-drive homer hit by Yogi Berra. The fan in the dark suit made a closed-eyes catch.

The 1955 American League batting champion, Al Kaline accepts his awards before a Tigers game. In his left hand he holds the coveted Silver Bat.

Kaline scores from third base on a wild pitch against the Texas Rangers in 1972. Pitcher Mike Paul awaits the throw from the catcher as umpire Ron Luciano maneuvers to make the call.

89

Karras, Alex

CARE-US (1935-), football player, was born in Gary, Indiana. At Emerson High, Alex made the all-state football team for three straight years. Though somewhat hesitant, Karras accepted an athletic scholarship to the University of Iowa. In 1957, he won the Outland Trophy as the nation's best lineman. Drafted by the Detroit Lions of the National Football League (NFL) in 1958, Karras also signed a contract as a professional wrestler for the off-season. A four-time All-Pro selection, Alex Karras soon became one of the finest defensive tackles in the NFL. He was suspended for the entire 1963 season by NFL Commissioner Pete Rozelle when he revealed he had bet on pro football games. He returned to the Lions the following year and played with them through the 1971 season. After his retirement, Karras appeared in movies and on television talk shows. He was later a commentator on *ABC Monday Night Football.*

Nearly all great athletes have determination and courage. Many also have a sense of humor. And sometimes, that sense of humor is as outsized as the athlete—as in the case of defensive lineman Alex Karras.

Karras generally had several tricks up his jersey to liven his hours, but he also had the talent to do his job well. He spent his entire playing career (1958-1971) with the Detroit Lions. Four times he was All-Pro.

Alex George Karras was born July 15, 1935, in Gary, Indiana, the third of four boys. His father was Greek and his mother Canadian. All of the boys were football players. The oldest brother, Lane, played for the Washington Redskins. Teddy served with the Pittsburgh Steelers, the Chicago Bears, and Detroit. Alex's younger brother, Paul, seemed headed for the pros. But he injured his knee playing for the University of Iowa and had to give up the game.

During his high school years, young Alex spent his summers working in the Gary steel mills. He did not care much for football, but he enjoyed basketball and baseball. However, his two older brothers had played at Emerson High, and Alex felt duty-bound to follow their lead. He did well, making the Indiana all-state team in his last three years of high school.

Football also made a college education possible for him. The University of Iowa offered an athletic scholarship, and Karras accepted. But he still preferred other sports.

He was rated as a fine prospect at first. But after a while, the Iowa coaches began to wonder about the fun-loving tackle.

As a freshman, Karras weighed 232 pounds. Before his sophomore season, he was up to 262. Coach Forest Evashevski was furious. And the battle had just begun.

"I hated the university, the coaches, and football," asserts Karras. "I was kicked off the team 17 times, put on probation twice, and suspended three times."

Karras had a strong dislike for the proctor in charge of his dorm. Late one night, he climbed on the shoulders of Alex Mish, a 285-pound lineman. They wrapped a basketball player's raincoat around them and knocked at the proctor's door. When the sleepy-eyed proctor opened the door, he was face-to-belly with a 10-foot goliath. The proctor, it is claimed, went screaming down the hall.

Despite his mischief and his dislike for football, Karras finished second in the 1957 vote for the Heisman Trophy. He did capture the Outland Trophy as the nation's best lineman.

A girl student once accepted his request for a date "just to see what the monster was like." A few months later, he and the coed, Joan Jergensen, were married.

The Detroit Lions were interested in the college all-star lineman. Karras was their number-one draft pick in 1958. He signed with Detroit general manager Nick Kerbawy for $8500.

But before he was ready for pro ball, Alex Karras had a few other ideas to try.

A Des Moines, Iowa, wrestling promoter signed him for the off-season for $25,000, billing him as "Crippler Karras." But before starting his short mat career, Alex Karras passed himself off as a shot-putter to get to the Balkan Games in Greece. It was a great chance to

Karras gets some quick refreshment as he watches the action from the sidelines.

Karras, Alex

Karras takes off after intercepting a pass against the Cleveland Browns.

Karras stops running back Dave Osbom for no gain in a 1970 contest against the Minnesota Vikings.

Karras remained a pretty tough cookie when his playing days were over. Here, Alex stars in the film Blazing Saddles.

get a free visit with his relatives.

Karras had fun in his early days with the Lions. He found a kindred spirit in Detroit quarterback Bobby Layne. Layne thought so much of the rookie that he made him his chauffeur. He called Karras "Tippy-Toe" for his method of filtering through the blockers.

But the relationship was short-lived. Layne was a jazz buff. He liked staying out all night and would often bribe the musicians to continue playing. The late hours did not bother him—but they left his "chauffeur," Karras, too groggy the next day.

At the end of his second season, Karras started to work seriously on his game. He got valuable tips on defensive line play from the line coach, Buster Ramsey.

At 6 feet, 2 inches, and 250 pounds, Alex Karras was not big for a defensive tackle. But he was nimble. He was quick in his attack on his target—the quarterback. Soon he was recognized as one of the best defensive tackles in the National Football League (NFL).

He never stopped his joking, or his habit of saying exactly what he thought—even though he frequently was wrong.

In the early 1960's, a new club, the Miami Dolphins, wanted Karras. "They'll never succeed," he stated after turning them down. But Miami developed into a first-rate ball club, and after only six years, they were world champions.

Even though he turned it down, the Miami offer helped Karras. The Lions decided to offer him a seven-year contract for $250,000.

He continued to make rash remarks. When Detroit played the Denver Broncos in 1967, Karras said there was no possible way the

Awaiting the snap from center, Karras lines up with the rest of the Lions' front four.

Broncos could win. "If they do," he promised, "I'll walk all the way back to Detroit."

Denver then proceeded to whip the Lions for the American Football League's (AFL) first win over the NFL. Karras had been kicked out of the game in the first two minutes. In the dressing room he showered, smoked two packs of cigarettes, and then he fainted. But he did not walk back to Detroit.

His biggest mistake came in 1962 when he talked about his bets on pro football games.

Pete Rozelle, commissioner of the National Football League, suspended Karras and Paul Hornung, the Green Bay back, for the entire 1963 season for gambling. Hornung accepted his suspension with grace. Alex Karras exploded in anger. Karras maintained that in Gary, his home town, everyone bet on sporting events. He said he should not be punished for doing what he was reared to do. He criticized Rozelle frequently.

At the same time, the Lions insisted that he give up his partnership in a lounge—The Lindell A.C., a hangout for Detroit athletes and their fans. Karras refused.

After he left Detroit, Washington wanted him. Karras made another rash remark, "Why should I want to go with Washington? I've played with a loser all my life. They can't win without a quarterback." The next year (1972), Washington went to the Super Bowl.

Off the field, Karras wears thick glasses. In 1959, he tried contact lenses in two exhibition games. "Strangely, I could see clearly for the first time," he said. "Still I played my two worst games."

To make up for his faulty eyesight, Alex Karras generally tackled by color. Once, though, Norm Van Brocklin, the Minnesota coach, confused him. The Vikings were wearing the same white jerseys as the Lions. After tackling his teammates three times, Karras asked for —and got—the Vikings to change to their darker home colors.

After his retirement in 1971, the colorful Karras turned to a show business career. He appeared on talk shows and television commercials, and he acted in several movies. In 1975 and 1976, Karras was a commentator on *ABC Monday Night Football* with Howard Cosell and Frank Gifford.

Kelly, John, Sr. (1889-1960),

rower, was born in Philadelphia, Pennsylvania. Practicing rowing for several hours a day, he also swam, boxed, and played football and basketball to keep in shape. Kelly captured the Championship single sculls in 1919 and 1920. The selection committee of the British Empire did not allow Kelly to participate in the 1920 Diamond Sculls at the British Henley Regatta, a major event in rowing. Stunned by the decision, the determined Kelly won a gold medal at the 1920 Olympics in the single sculls. He also won gold medals in the double sculls, with his cousin Paul Costello, at the 1920 and 1924 Olympic Games. In 1953, Kelly was chosen head of the National Association of Oarsmen. Kelly's daughter, Grace, became an actress and later the Princess of Monaco.

Kelly, Jack (John, Jr.) (1927-   ),

rower and son of John Kelly, Sr., was born in Philadelphia, Pennsylvania. Jack began rowing under his father's guidance at the age of seven, practicing on the Schuylkill River. At the University of Pennsylvania, Kelly played on the football team. Later, he worked solely on rowing, his father having bought the Vesper Boat Club in Philadelphia. Kelly won a number of Canadian and U.S. titles, including the 1947 Canadian sculling title and the Championship single sculls in 1946, 1948, 1950, and 1952. First competing in the Diamond Sculls at the British Henley Regatta in 1946, Kelly captured the event in 1947 and 1949. Kelly was awarded the 1947 James E. Sullivan Memorial Trophy as the nation's outstanding amateur athlete. Two years later in Amsterdam, he became the first American to win the European sculling championship. In 1956, Kelly won an Olympic bronze medal in the single sculls. Later, he coached the Vesper Club rowing and swimming teams. In 1970, he became president of the Amateur Athletic Union (AAU).

Champion rower John Kelly, Sr., shows his son, Jack, the award he won at the 1924 Olympic Games in Paris, France.

In 1920, a young Irish-American named John B. Kelly sought to enter the Diamond Sculls at the world-famous Henley Regatta, but his entry was ruled out. Twenty-seven years later, another John B. Kelly succeeded where the first had been denied. Not only did the second Kelly enter the event, he also emerged the victor by a decisive eight lengths over the one-and-one-quarter-mile course.

No official explanation was ever made to the first Kelly as to why his entry had been rejected. Off the record, he was told that the muscles he had developed as a bricklayer gave him an unfair advantage over his "gentlemen" competitors. The sport of rowing in those early years, so it seemed, was reserved for men who did not work with their hands. Deeply hurt and angry at being turned down, John Kelly vowed that someday he would avenge his hurt. After a wait of 27 years, his son and namesake, John B. Kelly, Jr., fulfilled that vow.

John Brendan Kelly, Sr., might truly be described as a self-made man. He was born in Philadelphia, Pennsylvania, on October 4, 1889. After attending public school, he

John Kelly, Sr., after his victory in the 1920 Olympics.

enrolled in evening classes at the Spring Garden Institute. During the day, he worked as an apprentice bricklayer.

When World War I started, he served in the U.S. Army, rising from private to lieutenant. After his discharge, he started his own construction business.

By the time of the Henley Regatta incident, the elder Kelly had already gained fame as an oarsman. In 1914, he won the Association singles and double sculls, and the Championship singles and quarter-mile singles in 1919 and 1920. He also soothed his anti-British feelings somewhat by defeating the long-time Canadian champion Bob Dibble. The Ameri-

Kelly, John Sr.
Kelly, Jack

Princess Grace of Monaco speaks with her brother, Jack Kelly, at the 1960 Olympic Games in Rome, Italy. Kelly was competing in the double sculls competition.

can nosed out Dibble by half a length in a stirring race held in sweltering 100-degree heat.

At the 1920 Olympics in Antwerp, Belgium, Kelly won the gold medal in single sculls. Then, with his cousin Paul Costello, he swept the doubles honors as well. His last notable victory was at the 1924 Olympics in Paris, France. There, he won a gold medal for the United States in the double sculls event, again teamed with Costello.

In later years John B. Kelly, Sr., ran for mayor of Philadelphia. Though defeated, he took his political defeat graciously. Kelly also served as president and member of numerous clubs and organizations. In 1953, he became head of the National Association of Oarsmen.

John B. Kelly, Jr., known to his friends as Jack, was born in Philadelphia, on May 24, 1927. At seven, the boy began his rowing career under his father's guidance. The older man often took his son to the Schuylkill River, and together they spent endless hours on the water. Determined to bring honor to the family through rowing, the father later bought the Vesper Boat Club in Philadelphia and its entire fleet for Jack's use.

The younger Kelly attended the University of Pennsylvania. Jack played center on the football team, behind the great Chuck Bednarik. But, at his father's urging, he quit the grid sport to concentrate wholly on rowing.

During the late 1940's, Jack Kelly dominated rowing in North America and was beaten only twice in competition. He captured a number of Canadian and U.S. titles, including the Canadian sculling title in 1947. He also scored wins in Swiss and Belgian events. At Amsterdam in 1949, he became the first American to win the European sculling championship. Among Kelly's other victories were the Association single sculls in 1946; the quarter-mile single sculls in 1950; and the Championship single sculls in 1946, 1948, 1950, and 1952.

His proudest victory in these years was his triumph in the Diamond Sculls at the Royal Henley Regatta in 1947. Kelly decisioned Carl Fronsdal of Norway and won by the easy margin of eight lengths. For that year's performance the

John Kelly, Sr. (right), helps his son, Jack, to a boat tent after the younger Kelly collapsed at the finish line in the 1948 Olympics. A heavy favorite, young Kelly was defeated in this semifinal single sculls race.

King Albert of Belgium congratulates John Kelly, Sr., after his victory in the single sculls at the 1920 Olympics.

young oarsman was awarded the James E. Sullivan Trophy, the highest honor bestowed by the Amateur Athletic Union (AAU). Two years later Jack duplicated his Diamond Sculls victory, finishing 100 yards ahead of his opponent.

Strange to say, the younger Kelly never captured an Olympic gold medal in rowing. In the Olympic competition in London in 1948, he lost in the semifinals. At Helsinki, Finland, in 1952, he was beaten in the second trial heat. At Melbourne, Australia, in 1956, he placed third in the final race to take a bronze. At Rome, Italy, in 1960, Kelly entered only the double sculls with Bill Knecht. But the two teammates were weakened from bouts of dysentery, and they finished a lowly fourth in the trial heat.

After his father died on June 20, 1960, Jack Kelly retired from active rowing competition to devote more time to the family business. He continued his interest in sports by coaching the Vesper Club's rowing and swimming teams. In 1970, he was elected president of the Amateur Athletic Union.

The annals of sport have few father-and-son combinations to equal the feats of the Kellys from Philadelphia. Between them, the two American oarsmen managed to capture most of the major titles in the world of sculling. For John Kelly, Sr., revenge was indeed sweet.

A thoughtful John Kelly, Sr., pauses during Olympic competition.

Eighteen-year-old Jack Kelly prepares for competition during the Peoples Regatta at Philadelphia, Pennsylvania. Kelly was the winner of five single sculling races in the event.

The 1920 Olympic gold medalist in single sculls, John Kelly, Sr.

Kelly, Leroy (1942-),

football player, was born in Philadelphia, Pennsylvania. The family lived near a park, and Leroy and his brother Pat spent a good deal of time there playing football, basketball, and baseball. A football star at Simon Gratz High School and an all-city shortstop, Leroy was recruited by Morgan State College in Baltimore. There, he was switched from quarterback to running back because his arm was not strong enough for major competition. The Cleveland Browns of the National Football League (NFL) picked him in the eighth round of the 1963 draft. Playing behind the legendary Jim Brown, Kelly was used chiefly as a punt and kickoff return specialist in 1964 and 1965. He became a starting running back in 1966 and promptly responded with three straight years of over 1000 yards rushing. His best year was 1968, when he gained 1239 yards. Kelly played in six Pro Bowl games and four NFL championship games. When he retired in 1974, he ranked fourth on the NFL all-time rushing list.

In 1966, Leroy Kelly replaced the retired Jim Brown as the top running back for the Cleveland Browns. He wasted little time in establishing himself. Each year from 1966-1968, he gained over 1000 yards rushing, leading the league in 1967 and 1968. Before retiring in 1974, he had become the fourth-leading rusher in National Football League (NFL) history.

Leroy Kelly was born on May 20, 1942, in Nicetown, Pennsylvania, on the south side of Philadelphia. His father worked in a chemical plant and played semi-pro baseball. Leroy's older brother Pat was a major-league outfielder.

Leroy was an all-round athlete at Simon Gratz High School, as his three older brothers had been.

Leroy and his brothers played a lot of baseball and football at Fern Hill, a nearby park. Says Kelly, "A lot of ghettos didn't have parks. We were lucky."

In football, he played both offense and defense and served as his team's punter and return specialist. But the talented young Kelly was at his best as a running quarterback. He had great confidence in his own ability, and so did his coach. Once, on fourth down with 12 yards to go from his own two-yard line, the coach signaled Kelly to run for it. He ran 98 yards for the touchdown.

Few universities were interested in Kelly. He had not taken a college preparatory course but had majored in auto mechanics.

Leroy Kelly enrolled at Morgan State College in Baltimore. Some of the Baltimore Colts used to watch Morgan State work out, and they often advised the players. Kelly was

After taking the hand-off, Kelly follows his blockers.

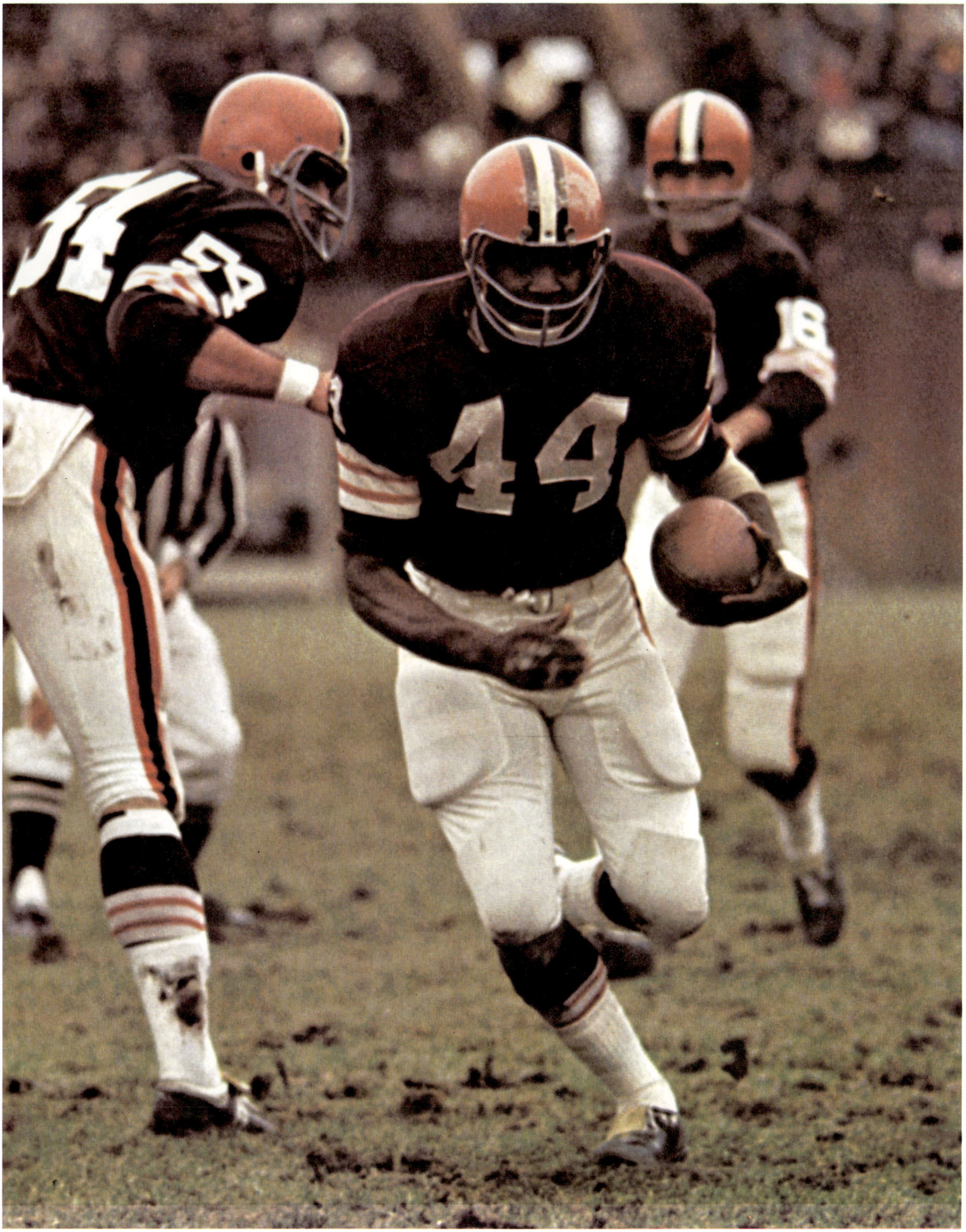

Kelly, Leroy

An official signals a touchdown after Kelly snags a pass in the end zone from Bill Nelsen. Kelly gained 127 yards in 17 carries and scored three touchdowns against the New Orleans Saints in this 1968 contest.

As he watches the game from the sidelines, Kelly takes a breather.

helped by former Indiana University star George Taliaferro. "He taught me to keep my eyes open going through the line and to seek out avenues of escape," says Kelly.

When he graduated from Morgan State, the pro scouts were as leery of him as the college scouts had been four years before. They felt that Kelly, at 188 pounds, was too light for a running back.

But Colt star Buddy Young kept touting Kelly to the pro clubs, claiming he was a second Jimmy Brown: "He's got all the same moves. He flies, cuts, never gives you a full piece of himself, keeps those feet close to the ground."

No American Football League (AFL) team drafted Kelly. And in the NFL he was only an eighth-round choice of the Cleveland Browns.

The Browns signed Kelly and brought him to Cleveland for a tryout. Coach Blanton Collier recalls, "He was too small. I said, 'Leroy, I wish you were bigger.'" Determined to make the professional ranks, Kelly said, "I'll be 200 the next time you see me." When he came back in the fall, he weighed 200 pounds.

In his early years with the Browns, Kelly was used chiefly as a punt-returner. He averaged 19 yards per return in 1964 and 15.6 yards in 1965, when he led the league. During that time, he was also used as a kickoff-returner.

In 1966, Kelly got his chance at the running back spot when Jim Brown retired. He responded by gaining 1141 yards and scoring 16 touchdowns.

Before the 1967 season, Kelly and several other Cleveland players decided to demand higher salaries. Having proven himself at running back, Kelly demanded a raise that was refused by the Cleveland management. He played under his old contract.

Because of his contract difficulties, he would have been out of a job at the end of the season if he had not performed well. "I was taking a big chance," Leroy said later. "It was lucky I stayed healthy."

Kelly was not only good that season, he was great. He topped the NFL in rushing yardage with 1205 and scored 13 touchdowns. The performance earned him a new four-year contract at more than $65,000 per year.

Avoiding Chris Hanburger of the Washington Redskins, Kelly skirts around end.

Kelly and Brown coach Blanton Collier review films of a game against the New Orleans Saints in 1968.

While Jim Brown was perhaps the greatest runner ever, Kelly was probably more versatile. A skilled blocker and pass receiver, he also continued to handle punt and kickoff returns after taking over the fullback spot.

In 1968, Leroy Kelly had his best season. He rushed for a career high of 1239 yards to lead the NFL for the second straight year. He averaged five yards a carry and led the league in rushing touchdowns (16) for the third year in a row. Kelly also topped the NFL in scoring that year with 120 points and a total of 20 touchdowns.

Kelly's career statistics reveal his great endurance. In his 10 years with the Browns, he gained 7274 yards in 1727 carries for a 4.2-yard average. He retired as the fourth-leading rusher in NFL history. He also scored 90 touchdowns and caught 190 passes. For his achievements, Kelly played in the Pro Bowl game six straight seasons.

In a game against the New York Jets, Kelly starts to cut in on a sweep.

Kelly scores a touchdown in a win over Dallas.

The accomplishments of his team are just as outstanding. During Kelly's career, the Browns played in four NFL championship games. In 1964, the Browns took the title by beating the Baltimore Colts, 27-0.

But there was one goal that escaped Kelly. "These things mean nothing compared with the Super Bowl," he once said. "I must play there before I'm through." The biggest disappointment of his brilliant career was that he never reached the Super Bowl.

101

Kelly, Red (Leonard) (1927-),

hockey player, was born in Simcoe, Ontario, Canada. As a youth, he developed into a good all-round player. Kelly was signed by the Detroit Red Wings for the 1947-1948 season. In his third year there as a defenseman, Kelly made the National Hockey League (NHL) All-Star second team. It started a 10-year stretch that saw him elected to the first team six times and the second team twice. His first-team berths included a string of five straight from 1951-1955. Kelly won the Lady Byng Trophy for sportsmanship combined with fine play in 1951, 1953, 1954, and 1961. His teams at Detroit won seven consecutive regular-season championships from 1949-1955 and captured four Stanley Cups—in 1950, 1952, 1954, and 1955. Kelly later played for the Toronto Maple Leafs. His teams there won four Stanley Cups, including three in a row from 1962-1964. A member of the Hockey Hall of Fame, he retired after the 1967 Cup playoffs. Kelly later coached the Los Angeles Kings and the Pittsburgh Penguins of the NHL. He was named coach of the Maple Leafs for the 1973-1974 season and spent four years at that post.

Versatility on and off the ice was the trademark of Leonard Patrick "Red" Kelly. For part of his 20 seasons in the National Hockey League (NHL), Kelly was an outstanding All-Star defenseman with the Detroit Red Wings. In another part of his hockey career, he performed as a first-class center with the Toronto Maple Leafs. Still later, he devoted his time to NHL coaching. During his athletic career, Red Kelly also served briefly as a Liberal Party member in the Canadian parliament.

Red Kelly was selected to hockey's Hall of Fame in recognition of his skillful play both as a defenseman and as a forward. Red built his greatest reputation as a defenseman, making the NHL All-Star first team six times in his first 10 seasons in the league and the second All-Star team twice. For five straight years, 1951 through 1955, he earned selection to the first team along with Montreal's Doug Harvey—considered by many as the finest rear guard ever to play in the NHL.

Kelly played defense in a far different manner than Harvey. Red was one of the first great rushing defenders. Coming up through the hockey ranks, he often played left wing and center and developed good offensive skills. Because of his scoring ability, first displayed in 1949-1950, Kelly was known as "Detroit's fourth forward." Red scored 15 goals that year and was selected to the NHL All-Star second team.

Victory accompanied Kelly

102

throughout his career in the NHL. During his 20 seasons in the big leagues, Red's teams failed to make the playoffs only once, when the Red Wings team of 1958-1959 finished in last place. While Kelly was playing for Detroit, the Red Wings captured seven straight regular-season championships and won four Stanley Cups—in 1950, 1952, 1954, and 1955. With Red in the lineup, Detroit also captured first place in 1957 regular-season play. After Kelly went to Toronto, the team captured four Stanley Cups—including three in a row from 1962-1964—and finished first during the 1963 regular season. Red retired as a player after Toronto's Cup victory in the spring of 1967. His 19 years in the playoffs equal Gordie Howe's all-time record for Cup appearances. Kelly played in 164 post-season games, more than any other man in hockey.

In the dressing room before Toronto takes on Montreal in a 1962 contest, center Red Kelly (left) tells team equipment manager Tom Naylor he wants his skates good and sharp.

Leonard Patrick Kelly was born on his father's farm in Simcoe, Ontario, on July 9, 1927. As a youngster, he was a staunch supporter of the Toronto Maple Leafs. There was no ice to skate on at his farm. So Red used to ride four miles on a pony owned by his father to reach the nearest frozen pond.

Red developed into a good all-round player, on both the forward line and defense. But in those days he was not an especially good skater. This apparently was the reason the Maple Leafs did not sign him in the late 1940's.

But Carson Cooper, a Detroit scout, thought Kelly had a lot to offer. He convinced the Red Wings to sign the redhaired young Irish-Canadian. Red reported to the Wings for the 1947-1948 campaign. Coach Tommy Ivan put him on a defensive back line with Bill Quackenbush, a perennial All-Star. "Play like Quackenbush does," Kelly was advised by a Detroit official. "Act like he does, learn to play his style." This was solid advice, for Quackenbush was not only a fine player, but an exceptionally clean one as well.

Mild-mannered Red became a good partner for Quackenbush. Then in 1949, the veteran defenseman was traded to Boston. In 1951, Kelly began his streak as a first-team All-Star choice. His old partner Quackenbush was likewise honored. That 1951 season also saw Red win the Lady Byng Trophy—awarded annually to the player judged to combine sportsmanship and gentlemanly conduct with superior playing ability. Kelly

103

Kelly, Red

Coach Kelly has to don ear muffs behind the Pittsburgh Penguin bench so that he won't hear the fans' abuse.

was to win the Lady Byng three more times (in 1953 and 1954 with the Red Wings and in 1961 with the Maple Leafs). Only one player in the history of the NHL ever won more than four Lady Byng awards. That was Frank Boucher, the great forward of the New York Rangers. In 1316 NHL contests, Red sat out a total of only 327 minutes with penalties—very little time in such a rough-and-tumble sport as hockey.

Kelly earned still another distinction. The league governors decided in 1954 to present an annual James Norris Memorial Trophy to the best defenseman. The first player to receive the award was Red Kelly.

In the 1953-1954 Stanley Cup championship effort of the Red Wings, Kelly scored 16 goals and 33 assists in 62 games during the regular season. He added five more goals in 12 playoff games.

With other Detroit players, Kelly slumped in 1959-1960. Partway through the season, he was suddenly traded to the New York Rangers. For once, Kelly was extremely angry. He refused to report to New York, saying he would rather retire from hockey. The Red Wings tried to explain to Red that he was traded to New York because he might eventually become the coach of the Rangers. But Red refused to budge.

Finally, Kelly agreed to report to the Toronto Maple Leafs, the club he originally had hoped to play for 13 years earlier. In 18 games with Toronto late in the 1959-1960 campaign, Red scored six goals. This matched the number he had scored in 50 games for Detroit before he was traded. In Toronto, Punch Imlach, the Leafs' coach and manager, moved Kelly to center ice on a fulltime basis. Red was on a line that had Frank Mahovlich at left wing. Then 22 years old, Mahovlich had shown the potential to emerge as a major hockey star. Red always had the capacity for making other players better by steadying them. The next year, with Kelly centering for him, Mahovlich scored 48 goals and was on the way

Kelly (Number 4) scores for the Toronto Maple Leafs against Detroit goalie Roger Crozier.

to becoming a great NHL star.

With the Leafs, Red Kelly had his three most productive offensive seasons. He scored 20 goals in 1961, a career high of 22 in 1962, and 20 again in 1963. In all, he scored 119 goals as a member of the Maple Leafs to go with the 162 goals he scored for Detroit.

In 1967, Kelly left the Maple Leafs to become head coach of the Los Angeles Kings expansion team. He took a team considered the least talented of the six new clubs and steered it into second place, one point behind season champion Philadelphia. The next year, he coached the Kings to a fourth-place finish and another playoff spot. Then he took over the coaching reins of the Pittsburgh Penguins and led that club to second place in the West Division. In 1970-1971, the Penguins dropped to sixth place. But the following year, they were back in the playoffs with a fourth-place finish.

Midway through the 1972-1973 NHL season, Kelly was dismissed as Pittsburgh coach and succeeded by Ken Schinkel. But before the 1973–1974 season, he was hired as head coach by the Toronto Maple Leafs, his old team. Kelly coached the club through the 1976-1977 season.

Kidd, Billy (1943-),

skier, was born in Burlington, Vermont. From the time he was very young, his family encouraged him to become a ski racer. He attended the University of Colorado, where he met Bob Beattie, who strongly influenced him—especially when Bob became the U.S. national ski team coach in 1961. Billy won the 1964 Olympic silver medal in the slalom at Innsbruck, Austria, becoming the first U.S. man ever to claim a medal in Olympic or World Championship competition. Kidd also earned a bronze medal in the combined standings. In 1964, he won the U.S. national giant slalom title and was named the athlete of the year by U.S. skiers. After recovering from leg and ankle injuries, Kidd ranked seventh in World Cup standings in 1968, the highest finish among U.S. skiers. In 1970, he became the first, and to date, the only American man to win a gold medal in the World Championships. Kidd then turned professional and joined the International Ski Racers Association. He won the world professional title in 1970. Following injury-ridden seasons in 1971 and 1972, Billy Kidd retired from competitive skiing.

Billy Kidd recalls the day in 1960 when he left New York for the junior national skiing championships in Colorado. Walking through the airport lobby with his skis on his shoulders, he was mistaken for a pole-vaulter. Such a thing could not happen today. In the last two decades the sport of skiing has become widely known in America. And the man largely responsible for its present popularity is Billy Kidd.

In 1964, Kidd became the first American to capture an Olympic medal for Alpine skiing. In 1970, he became the first American to win a gold medal at the Fédération Internationale de Ski (FIS) World Championships, taking first place in the combined (slalom, giant slalom, and downhill). Since that time, no American man has matched either feat. It cost him years of hard work, broken bones, sprained ankles, and a bad back. But Billy Kidd reached the top and became an American ski hero.

William Kidd was born in Burlington, Vermont, on April 13, 1943. His family owned a lodge in nearby Stowe, Vermont. He practically grew up on skis there. By 1960, 17-year-old Billy finished second in the junior national slalom championship behind another young skier who later shared fame with him, Jimmie Heuga. After his win, Billy Kidd's family encouraged his racing. He then received outstanding technical training and support from the coaches of the Mt. Mansfield Ski Club during his years in junior competition.

After high school, Kidd decided to attend the University of Colorado in Boulder. Another New Englander was then coaching its ski team. The coach was Bob Beattie. Beattie's successful guidance of the Colorado ski team to two National Collegiate Athletic Association (NCAA) championships had earned him the job of U.S. national ski team coach. Beattie and Kidd became good friends. And the coach had a great influence on Kidd's progress in skiing.

In 1972, Kidd recalled the problems he faced in perfecting his skill. "One of the reasons I was a good ski racer was because I had a chronically sprained ankle. I had to figure out how to ski race without falling down because, as soon as I'd fall down, I'd sprain my ankle. When I sprained my ankle, I couldn't race for three or four weeks.

"Another thing," Kidd continued, "was that I was going to school at the same time I was racing. I didn't have eight hours a day, ten months a year, to practice. So, I had to figure things out about how to make the most efficient turn, how to get myself psyched up for a race, how to go through a season and peak at the right moment, and how to get the most out of my training—so that in two hours a day, I could compete with Karl Schranz or Jean-Claude Killy, who were skiing ten hours a day.

"I thought about skiing probably more than most people in ski racing. I thought about how skis are made and why, and thought about how to take advantage of my skis. I thought about how to go through a training program and how to approach my year psychologically."

The great mental preparation, combined with years of experience in national competitions, paid off for Billy Kidd. But it took time—and that time was filled with disappointments, winless seasons, almost constant pain from his chronically sprained ankle, and little recognition. But Billy Kidd was dedicated and had faith in his abilities. So did Bob Beattie.

On February 8, 1964, America —after almost 30 years of trying to win a place in international ski competition—finally found its hero. Billy Kidd, then 20, placed second in the slalom at the most honored of all ski events, the Winter Olympics, held that year in Innsbruck, Austria. In sixth place after the first run, Kidd poured it on for his second slalom run. He ended up with a silver medal—the first Alpine medal ever earned by an American in Olympic or World Championship competition. Jimmie Heuga was third in the slalom for a bronze medal to add to America's glory.

Here is Billy Kidd in the giant slalom race at the 1964 Winter Olympics. He roared down the hill for a seventh-place finish.

Kidd, Billy

A happy Billy Kidd rides the shoulders of his teammates after winning the Alpine combined gold medal at the World Championships in Val Gardena, Italy.

Holding the first annual "Kidd Cup," Billy admires the three-foot-high trophy given to him for his "outstanding contribution to American competitive skiing."

Kidd (left) shows off the silver medal he won for the men's slalom at the 1964 Winter Olympics. He poses with bronze medalist Jimmie Heuga of the U.S.

Kidd was also seventh in the Olympic giant slalom and 16th in the downhill—earning him the bronze medal in the combined standings.

In 1964, the pain of the long period of preparation was forgotten. Billy collected two Olympic medals and a U.S. national giant slalom title. He was named athlete of the year by U.S. skiers. He also raced to victory in the famous Roch Cup at Aspen, Colorado.

He won the Roch Cup again in 1965. This time he took all three events (slalom, giant slalom, and downhill) against the best racers in America.

In 1966, Billy Kidd went back to Europe with the U.S. team. Again he showed the Europeans that he was a man to respect. He won the slalom and the combined at Hindeland, West Germany, and the giant slalom and the combined at Adelboden, Switzerland. But bad luck struck when he was injured and forced to undergo surgery on his ankle.

During the summer he broke his leg while training at Portillo, Chile, site of the 1966 World Championships. Kidd was out of competition throughout 1967 while he recovered.

But that setback did not stop him. He came back in 1968 with an impressive seventh in the World Cup standings. That was the top U.S. finish that season. And it remains one of the best U.S. World Cup performances on record. He won the World Cup slalom at Aspen, defeating Jean-Claude Killy, among others, for the first U.S. victory in World Cup competition.

That winter, Kidd was disqualified for falling during the Olympic slalom at Grenoble, France. But he was fifth in the giant slalom. His second run time during the event even beat that of the winner, Jean-Claude Killy.

In 1969, he tied for 13th place in the World Cup rankings. Billy Kidd highlighted his season with a victory in the Cup slalom at Squaw Valley, California. The 5-foot, 8-inch, 155-pound skier had become the team leader for the United States. And the 1970 World Championships in Val Gardena, Italy, were just around the corner.

Kidd's long series of injuries had kept him on the edge of success for six years since his silver medal at Innsbruck. Observers questioned whether the 26-year-old racer still had the talent to win. But Val Gardena turned out to be Billy Kidd's show.

He began the week in Italy by taking a bronze medal in the slalom despite a painful back injury that forced him to wear a brace. Then he came back from a plodding first run in the giant slalom with a

On his way to winning a gold medal in the Alpine combined at the 1970 Alpine World Ski Championships, Kidd passes a gate in the giant slalom event. Kidd became the first American male to win a gold medal in the event.

second run that moved him from 30th to 15th place. Next was the downhill. He placed fifth, but fifth was good enough for a gold medal in the combined—the first gold medal in international Alpine competition for America.

With his gold medal securely around his neck, Billy Kidd announced at Val Gardena that he was turning professional. Kidd was joining the International Ski Racers Association, which had been organized by Bob Beattie.

Billy won $15,000 on his brief 1970 pro tour. He collected the world professional title, which gave him another first—no other skier had won both the world amateur and professional titles in one season.

The 1971 pro season was disappointing. Kidd finished 12th. In 1972, he ended up 18th. His skiing had been hampered again by that bad ankle. But it was more than his ankle that undermined his performance. He had little chance to practice.

Billy Kidd had signed several contracts with ski firms to promote their products. This commercial obligation took a great deal of time. It paid well but hurt his skiing.

In 1973, he gave up competitive skiing to devote full time to his businesses. He had married and was living in Steamboat Springs, Colorado. Kidd lives there today, serving as a director of the local ski area and as an advisor and representative for several firms. As a member of the President's Sports Council of Physical Fitness, he works to promote the sport of skiing.

Billy Kidd said, "I'll be helping racers by getting more people interested in skiing. This isn't something you can put your finger on to determine how much I'm doing to make skiing grow or how many more people I'm getting interested in racing. . . . I am being somewhat selfish about it, because there's nothing sooner forgotten than a sports hero. I've got a couple of years to do something while I'm not just Billy Kidd, average citizen. Right now I can do something with skiing in general and promote the sport."

Killebrew, Harmon

KILL-UH-BREW (1936-   ), baseball player, was born in Payette, Idaho. He was a 12-letter man in high school and an all-national scholastic quarterback in football. While batting an amazing .847 in the semi-pro Idaho-Oregon Border League, Killebrew was signed by the Washington Senators of the American League as a bonus player in 1954. In his first full season with Washington, 1959, Killebrew drove in 105 runs. He also hit 42 homers to tie for the league honors. For the next decade with the Senators and the Minnesota Twins, he became one of the top power hitters in the game. He won the American League's Most-Valuable-Player award in 1969, when he batted .276 with a league-leading 49 home runs and 140 runs batted in (RBI). He made the All-Star team 11 times and led the American League in homers six times. After spending the 1975 season with the Kansas City Royals, Killebrew retired, ranking fifth on the all-time home-run list with 573.

They say that lightning never strikes twice in the same place, but it did for owner Clark Griffith of the Washington Senators.

Early in his career, Griffith unwillingly shelled out a $100 bonus for a young Idaho pitcher named Walter Johnson. The year was 1906. Johnson went on to become one of baseball's all-time greats.

Nearly 50 years later, Griffith signed another unknown young player from Idaho. Griffith paid Harmon Killebrew $30,000. Like the $100 bonus in 1906, it was a good investment.

The year was 1954. The aging Griffith was thinking about his shortage of good hitting infielders. The U.S. Senator from Idaho, Herman Welker, suggested that Griffith send a scout to watch Harmon Killebrew. Killebrew was a 17-year-old semi-pro player in the Idaho-Oregon Border League. Griffith sent scout Ossie Bluege to Idaho for a look. Bluege's report on the youngster was hard to believe. Killebrew was batting an incredible .847. Bluege described him as "like a right-handed Mickey Mantle." Clark Griffith came up with $30,000 for the young player, the first one he had signed under the newly established bonus rule.

Harmon Clayton Killebrew was born June 29, 1936, in Payette, Idaho. In high school he was a 12-letter man and an all-national scholastic quarterback. When Griffith signed him, he joined the Senators right away. Under the bonus rule, Killebrew would have to remain in the big leagues for at least two years. The imposed major-league sentence proved hard on Killebrew. He was not ready for such rugged competition. In 1955, the Senators put Killebrew into 38 games at second and third base. He batted just .200 that year. His .222 average for 44 games the fol-

Killebrew slugged 573 home runs during his career, placing him fifth on the all-time list.

110

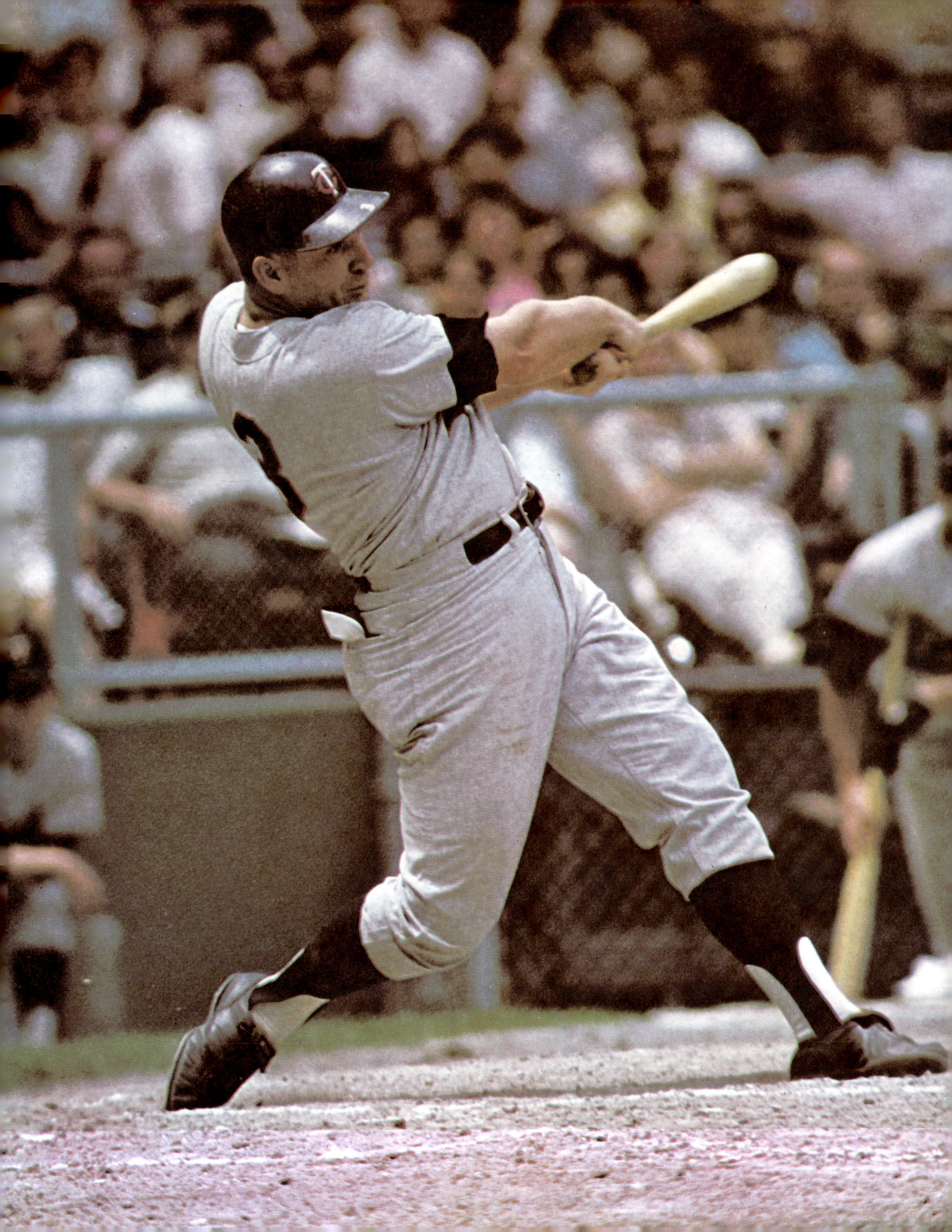

Killebrew, Harmon

lowing year was not much better.

It looked as if "Old Fox" Griffith had made a mistake on the muscular marvel from Idaho. Midway through the 1956 season, Griffith sent Killebrew to the South Atlantic (Sally) League, where at least he would get a chance to play regularly. After two and a half seasons in the minors, Killebrew returned to Washington in 1959. Now he was an accomplished slugger. Killebrew tied for the most home runs in the league that year with 42, and he recorded 105 runs batted in (RBI). It was the first of nine straight seasons in which Killebrew hit 25 or more home runs.

In 1960, the Senators' last year in Washington, Killebrew hit 31 home runs. And his batting average was up to .276. A year's experience had taught him to cut down on his swing, and he had learned how to have fewer strikeouts. During 1959 and 1960, Killebrew was part of baseball's most powerful "Murderer's Row," along with Roy Sievers, Jim Lemon, and Bob Allison. In 1959 alone, the four men hit 126 homers. But the Senators still finished the season in their usual bottom spot.

By 1961, Calvin Griffith, Clark's son, had decided the Senators could no longer make a profit in Washington. He moved the team to Minneapolis, Minnesota. They became the "Twins," after the "Twin Cities" of Minneapolis and St. Paul. By this time, Killebrew had become the team's most important player. He belted 46 homers that year, drove in 122 runs, and batted .288. He was now a legitimate star. Playing third base, first base, and the outfield that year, Killebrew made the All-Star team at each position later in his career.

In 1962, 1963, and 1964, Killebrew led the American League in homers—hitting 48, 45, and 49. In those three years he batted in 333 runs.

The Twins finally won a pennant in 1965, five years after they had left Washington. Oddly, it was not one of Killebrew's best years. He "slumped" to 25 homers and 75 RBI's. The Twins lost the World Series to the Los Angeles Dodgers in seven games. Harmon did well, batting .286.

The following year, Killebrew got back to the business of hitting homers. He hit 39 in 1966, then tied for the league lead again with 44 in 1967. In 1968, a freak injury threatened to end his great career.

Playing first base in the 1968 All-Star Game, Killebrew tore a muscle in his left leg when he stretched for a low throw. During the off-season, Harmon worked to build up his injured leg. He came back to have his greatest season in 1969. He played in all 162 games for the Twins, pounding out a

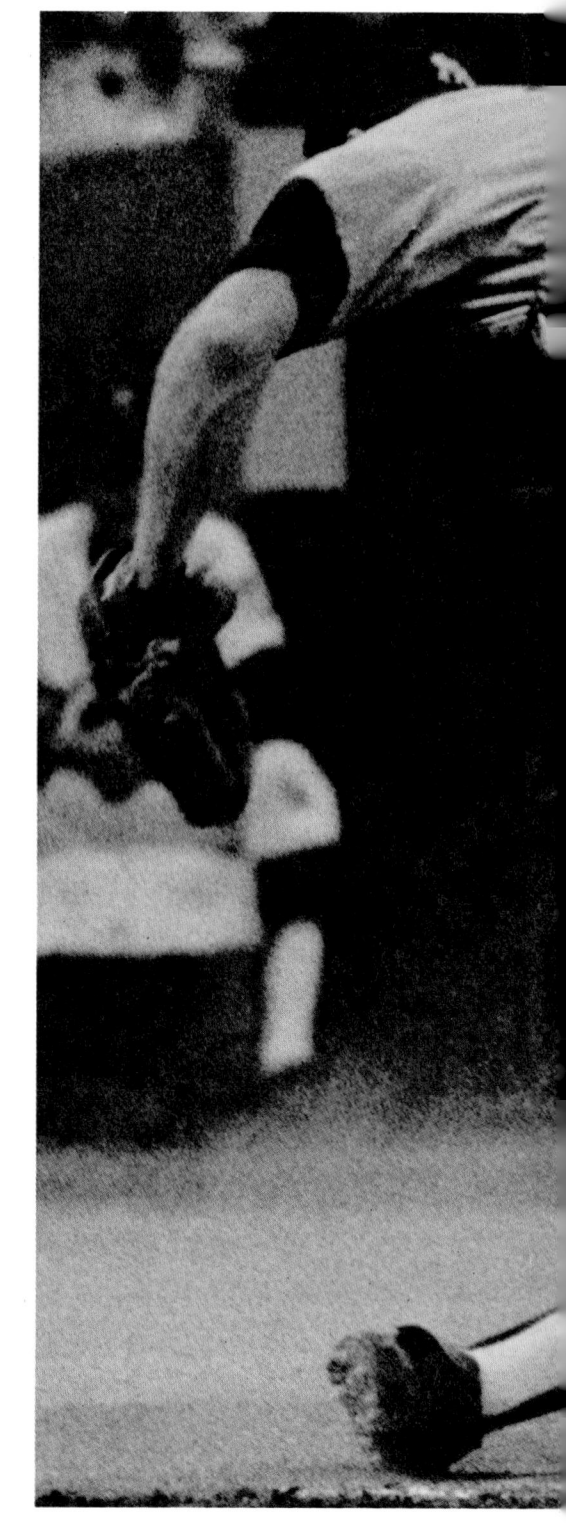

*Catcher Thurman Munson of the New
York Yankees is upended by
Killebrew on a safe slide at the plate.*

Killebrew, Harmon

Killebrew awaits the peg as Yankee second baseman Bobby Richardson races down the first-base line with arms raised to protect himself.

league-leading 49 homers and 140 RBI's. He won his first and only Most-Valuable-Player award.

Killebrew slammed 41 homers and drove in 113 runs in 1970. The following year, he collected a league-leading 119 RBI's.

After playing three more years for Minnesota, Killebrew joined the Kansas City Royals in 1975. He retired at the season's end with a lifetime total of 573 home runs, placing him fifth on the list of all-time leaders.

Killebrew's home-run percentage (home runs per time at bat) was 7.3. Only the immortal Babe Ruth had a higher percentage. Harmon Killebrew hit more than 40 homers in eight different major-league seasons. He won or shared six American League home-run titles and led the league in RBI's three times. He had come a long way from his early years in Idaho.

Calvin Griffith made an interesting remark about the slugger's success. "The best thing going for Harmon Killebrew," Griffith said in 1962, "is his level head. His early publicity would have gone to a lot of kids' heads. I talked about it when he was 21, and he told me, 'Mr. Griffith, you'll never have to worry; I'll never change.'

"And you know, he never did. He's the most appreciative player I ever met. I've never seen him refuse to sign an autograph, and he never complains."

Clark Griffith would have been proud of how his big bonus player turned out.

Jubilant Minnesota players douse slugger Harmon Killebrew with champagne following their pennant-clinching victory over Washington in 1965.

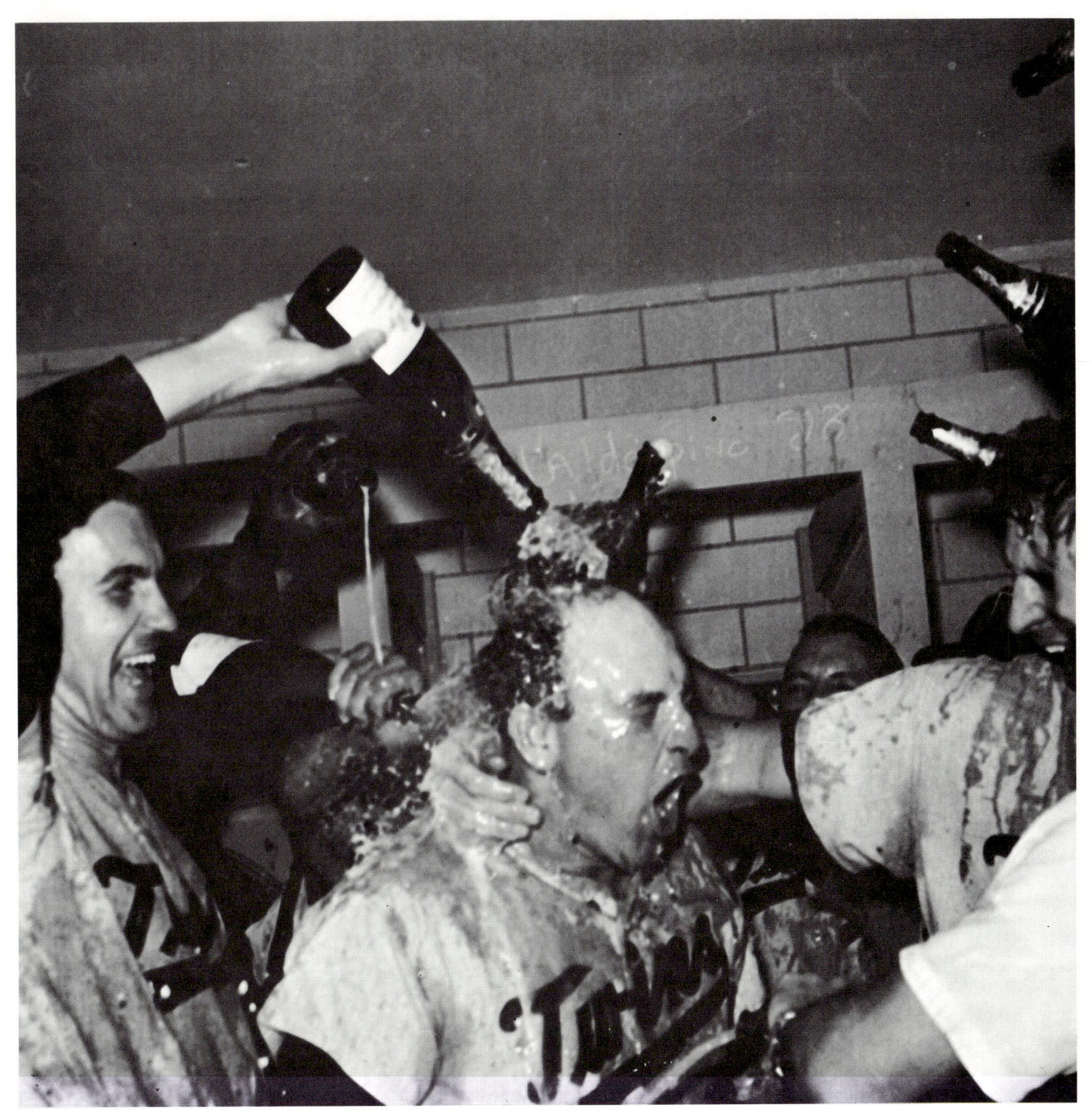

Killy, Jean-Claude

ZHAHN-CLAWD KEY-LEE (1943-), skier, was born in Saint-Cloud, France. When he was three, his family moved to the resort town of Val d'Isère, where Killy learned to ski. In 1959, he started training with the French national team and began to perfect the technique that would later make him famous. Competing in the 1964 Olympic Games at Innsbruck, Austria, he managed only fifth place in the giant slalom. The following year was the turning point in Killy's career. In 1965 and 1966, Killy won the World Championship combined titles. The first year of the World Cup competition, 1967, Killy won five downhill races, three slaloms, and four giant slaloms to finish well ahead of everyone in the point standings. Killy won three gold medals in Alpine skiing at the 1968 Olympics, becoming the second skier ever to do so. He retired from amateur competition after his second World Cup championship in 1968. Jean-Claude Killy returned to skiing as a professional in 1972 and captured the pro title. He retired from the professional tour in 1974.

In 1946, Robert Killy and his family moved from Saint-Cloud, outside Paris, to Val d'Isère, France. Skiing in this resort town was almost as routine as sleeping and eating for the children who lived there. And it became so for Robert Killy's children, too. At three, Jean-Claude Killy strapped on his first pair of skis and began schussing his way to fame.

By the time he was eight, Jean-Claude was skiing 12 long runs each day and had won his first race. At 10, he captured all three events in a regional junior meet against racers two and three years older than he. Enjoying the victory and the resulting attention, the young skier decided to stay with the sport.

That was 1953. Fifteen years later, he matched the feat of Toni Sailer by winning all three Alpine medals during the 1968 Winter Olympics in Grenoble, France. Jean-Claude Killy became the uncontested world champion. He was recognized (along with Sailer and Karl Schranz) as one of the very best skiers of all time.

Those 15 years held many ups and downs for Killy. Conflicts between his parents resulted in his being sent away to a school far from the ski slopes. Killy was miserable. His low spirits and frail condition contributed to an illness that forced him off skis for more than a year.

At 13, he began skiing again. During the next few years, he tried to make up for lost time. But later, when training with the French B team, Killy suffered a broken leg.

Jean-Claude breezes past the finish line for another victory.

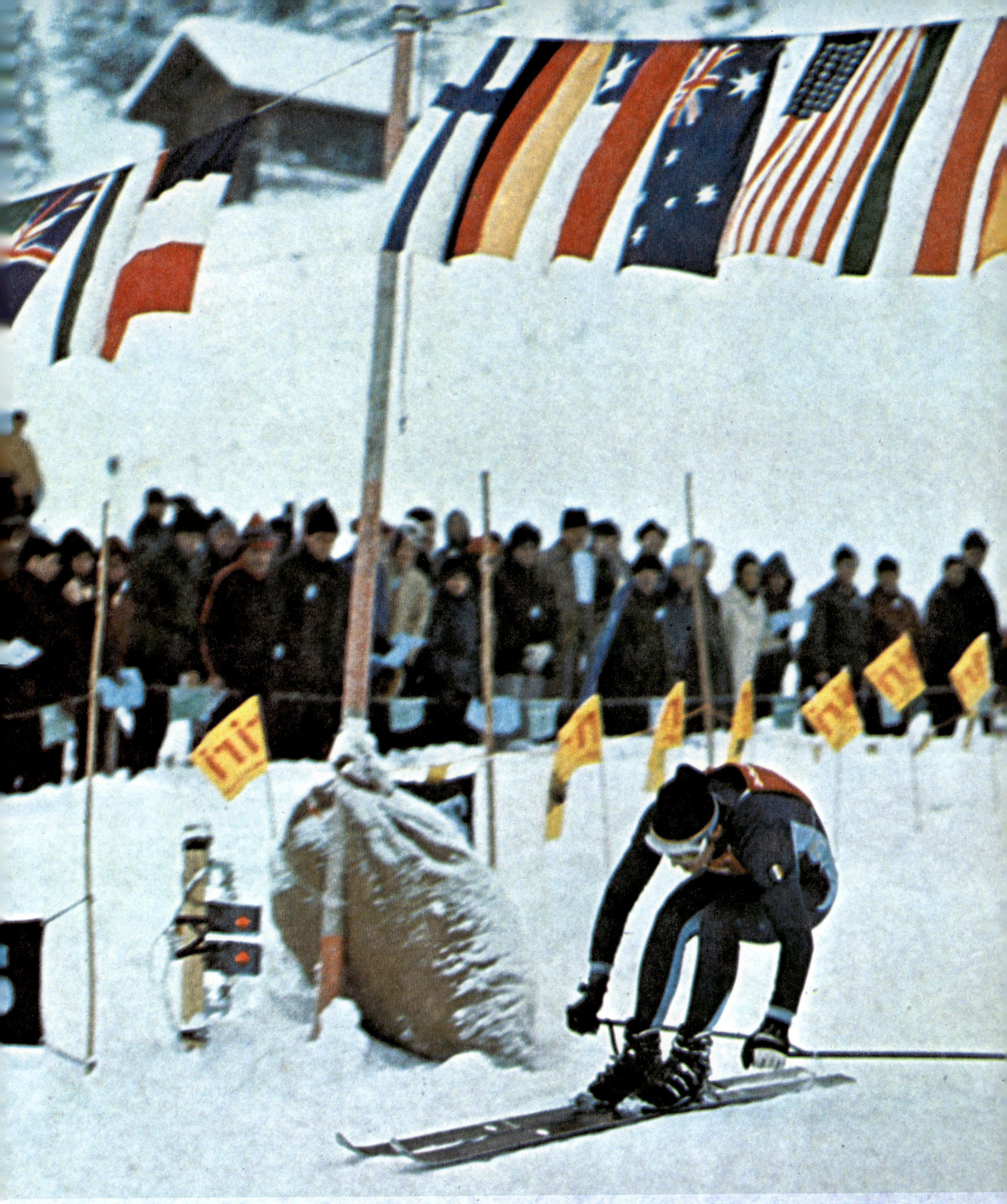

Killy, Jean-Claude

At Franconia, New Hampshire, in 1967, Killy wins the men's slalom in the North American Alpine Championships.

His mouth agape, Killy races to victory in the giant slalom of the World Series of Skiing at Vail, Colorado, in 1967.

Determined to race, he stayed off skis for only three months. Killy's several victories that year (1959) earned him a spot on the French "hopeful" squad. He quit school to devote all his time to skiing.

Training with the French national team, Killy developed an ability to imitate the best techniques of each of the outstanding skiers. He combined these techniques into his own unique and successful style. Soon, he was the one being imitated.

By 1961, the 18-year-old Jean-Claude was promoted to the French A team. Though he was still perfecting his technique, he continued winning races. He was heralded as the French star of the future. Then he broke his leg again —this time just before the 1962 World Championships. He was forced to watch the meet in Chamonix, France, on crutches rather than skis.

The next season he suffered from another illness, which led to a mediocre year. He was trying to prepare for the upcoming 1964 Winter Olympics at Innsbruck, Austria. But those Games were a disaster for him. He was eliminated

Killy leans inward while taking a gate during a slalom run.

At the 1968 Olympics in Grenoble, France, Killy flies through the air en route to a gold medal victory in the downhill.

Killy waves to the crowd after winning the gold medal in the giant slalom at the 1968 Olympics. At left is Heinrich Messner of Austria, who captured the bronze medal. At right is silver medalist Willy Favre of Switzerland.

Shown winning his second gold medal in the 1968 Olympics, Killy displays great balance.

from both the slalom and downhill races, and he managed only a fifth place in the giant slalom. Poorly prepared skis and an intestinal disease, amebic dysentery, sabotaged his performance that year.

Killy had recovered by the following season, and his luck began to change. At the famous Hahnenkamm in Kitzbühel, Austria, he defeated the once-thought unbeatable Austrian Karl Schranz by more than three seconds in the slalom run. The points from this race, added to the points he earned in the downhill and giant slalom, won him the coveted Hahnenkamm combined.

Although he had some conflicts with French coach Honoré Bonnet in the winter of 1965, Killy still managed some victories—including the Lauberhorn. He was well prepared for the 1966 World Championships held in August in Portillo, Chile.

In his most enjoyable victory, Jean-Claude captured the World Championship downhill in Portillo—his first big triumph in that event. He was fifth in the giant slalom and first in the combined. He was ready for the 1967 season.

Killy, Jean-Claude

At a 1972 press conference in Denver, Colorado, Jean-Claude Killy announces his return to skiing as a professional.

Making a comeback as a professional in 1973, Killy skis to victory in a race at Mt. Snow, Vermont.

It was the first season of World Cup competition. The relaxed Frenchman won all five of the downhills, three of the seven slaloms and four of the five giant slaloms on the circuit. He ended up with the maximum number of points possible—over 100 more than his nearest competitor. His domination of all three Alpine events was matchless. The World Cup victory started him thinking about the Winter Olympics in 1968. No one had won all the Olympic Alpine events since Toni Sailer's feat in 1956. Killy realized he had a good chance to grab the three gold medals. Jean-Claude was probably the best-prepared competitor at the 1968 Olympics in Grenoble. Although he had won only one World Cup title before the Games, he was mentally and physically ready for the ultimate contest. And he had the best equipment available. On Sailer's recommendation, Killy took a few days away from skiing before the Olympics. That short rest had excellent results.

He won his first Olympic gold medal in the downhill, defeating teammate Guy Perillat by 8/100 of a second. The win came despite the fact that the careful wax job had worn off Killy's skis before the race started. Then came the giant slalom. Killy won his second gold medal by a margin of more than two seconds.

The slalom was the final event at Grenoble. The weather was bad, with fog drastically limiting the range of sight. Killy had a good first run, but 14 racers were within a second of his time. During the second run, visibility was even worse. It was announced that Karl Schranz had beaten Killy's combined time on the basis of that second heat. Schranz claimed the Olympic gold medal—the only international trophy that had eluded him during his outstanding career. But the jury finally determined that the Austrian had missed a gate on the second course, and he was disqualified. So, Killy won three gold medals. In doing so, he had proven himself one of the most determined, able, and cool competitors ever to put on skis.

He finished the 1968 season with his second World Cup trophy and retired from amateur skiing. Killy then signed with American sport promoter Mark McCormack. By putting his name to cars, skis, ski boots, ski wear, and a television race series, he netted a figure rumored at around $1 million. He was even featured in a full-length movie, *Snow Job*.

In November 1972, Jean-Claude Killy got bored with his commercial life. The flash of popularity and fame had begun to fade. Most of all, he said, he missed the mountains.

He joined the International Ski Racers Association and competed on the U.S. professional circuit. During the early matches of the season, the dual slalom, head-to-head format of pro racing was physically difficult for him. But after 24 competitions, Killy became accustomed to the bone-crushing strain. He won the pro title and more than $68,000. The same style, skill, and cool that had gained him so many victories made him a world champion again.

In 1974, at the age of 29, Killy left the professional circuit. He had accomplished nearly everything that could be accomplished on skis. With his remarkable performances and great courage, he had earned himself a lasting place in skiing history.

Killy, who turned from skiing to auto racing, sits in his Porsche 911T before time trials at a 1968 race in Monza, Italy. Killy turned in the 19th-fastest qualifying time.

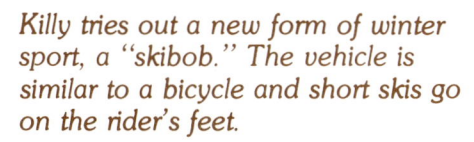

The great Killy coasts down a hill.

Killy tries out a new form of winter sport, a "skibob." The vehicle is similar to a bicycle and short skis go on the rider's feet.

Seeming to be racing his shadow, Jean-Claude Killy swoops down the side of an Alpine glacier. He is shown making his escape with a quarter-million dollars of stolen money in a scene from a 1971 movie, Snow Job. Killy starred in the film when he turned professional.

121

Kilmer, Billy (1939-),

football player, was born in Topeka, Kansas. Before attending the University of California at Los Angeles (UCLA), Kilmer was planning for a professional career in baseball or basketball. He decided to play football after receiving a scholarship. He was selected as an All-America running back in his senior year at UCLA. Kilmer was the first draft pick of the San Francisco 49'ers of the National Football League (NFL) in 1961. He soon came into his own as director of Red Hickey's 49'er shotgun offense. On December 5, 1962, a near-fatal auto accident almost ended Kilmer's career. He missed the 1963 and 1965 seasons entirely and was eventually selected by the New Orleans Saints in the expansion draft of 1967. He was traded to the Washington Redskins in 1971, when George Allen took over as head coach. A masterful field general, Kilmer led the Redskins to the postseason playoffs five times between 1971 and 1976, and to the Super Bowl following the 1972 season.

Perhaps one of sports' greatest comeback stories is that of quarterback Bill Kilmer. Kilmer's career nearly ended when he was badly injured in an auto accident December 5, 1962, when he was with the San Francisco 49'ers.

Yet, in the 1971 season, his passing led the Washington Redskins into the playoffs for the first time since 1945. The next season, he propelled them into the Super Bowl, where they were beaten by Miami, 14-7.

William Orland Kilmer was born September 5, 1939, in Topeka, Kansas. He grew up in Azusa, California, and starred in sports at Citrus High School. There, he set several basketball scoring records. Football was not Kilmer's game when he was young. "I was never a winner in football, and in my senior year in high school, I vowed I'd never set foot on a football field again," he said. "I was set to play pro baseball or basketball. But I changed my mind after Red Sanders [UCLA football coach] offered me a scholarship and a chance to play tailback, where I could run, throw, and kick."

Sanders died before Kilmer started to college. But at the University of California at Los Angeles (UCLA) Bill enjoyed playing football. The UCLA Bruins had a fine season (7-2-1) in Kilmer's senior year. The opposition never knew whether Kilmer would run or pass. Leading the University Division of the National Collegiate Athletic Association (NCAA) in total offense, he was named as an All-America running back.

"I was set on a baseball career, though," said Kilmer. "My grandfather started taking me to games in

Kilmer receives undivided attention as he calls a play in the Washington Redskin huddle.

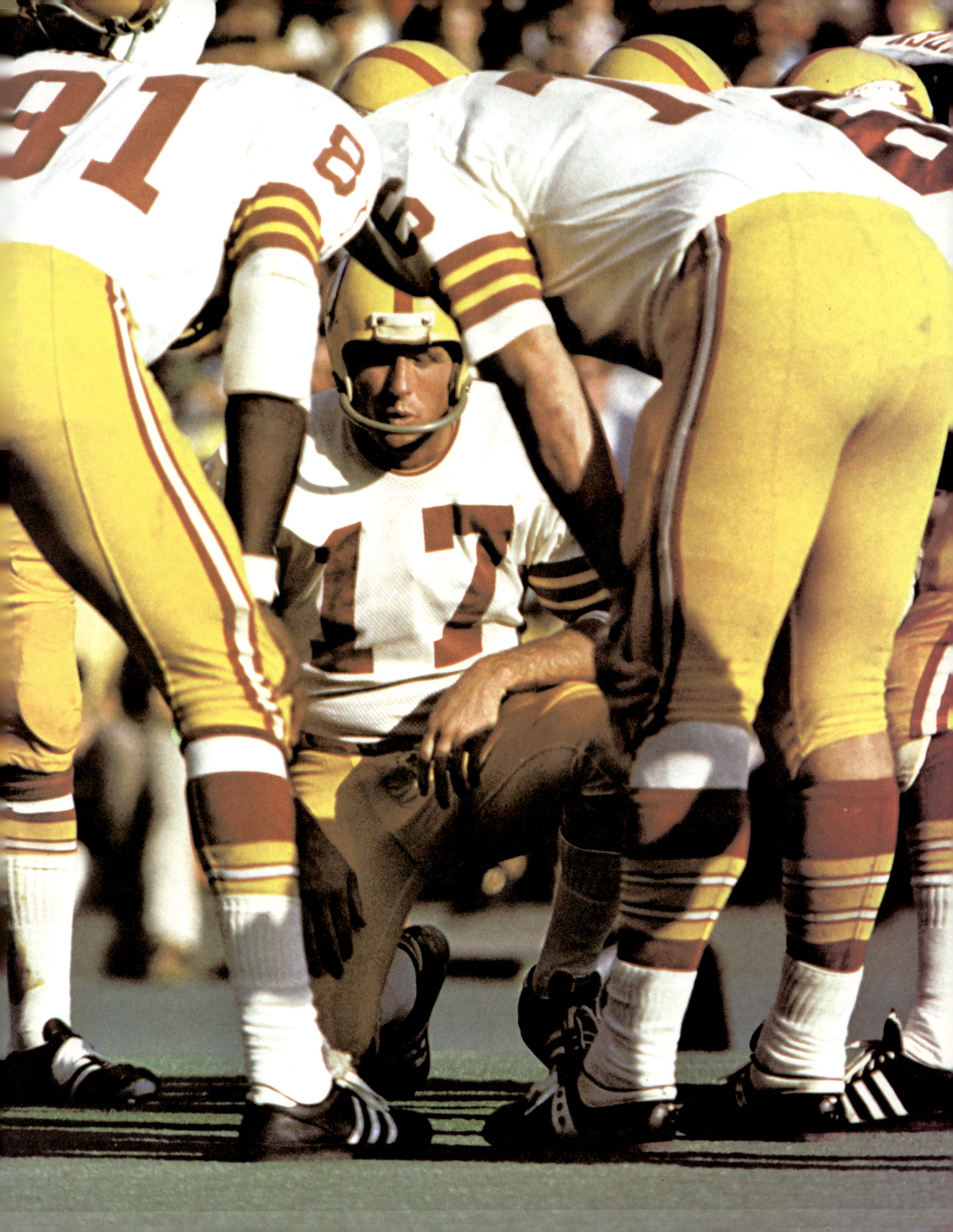

Kilmer, Billy

The Los Angeles Rams pour on the pressure, but Kilmer gets ready to hit his receiver during a 1971 Redskins-Rams contest.

Los Angeles when I was a tot. I always wanted to play pro ball." But Kilmer was drafted by the 49'ers in the first round. "If they thought that much of me," said Billy, "I had to see just how good I was myself."

At first, he seemed to be a misfit in pro football. He could not run as well as the running backs. He could not pass like the other National Football League (NFL) quarterbacks. And specialists handled the kicking. At 6 feet and 200 pounds, he did not even have the right build for a quarterback. But what he *could* do was compete. Seldom had pro football seen such a competitive quarterback. He loved the uncertainty of the life of a pro football player. He gave everything he had to the game. Then, he came into his own as director of Red Hickey's 49'er shotgun offense. He did the running, John Brodie did the passing. And then tragedy struck.

It happened while Bill was returning from a three-day hunting trip. He was driving up Bayshore highway, south of San Francisco. Around 8 P.M., he fell asleep at the wheel. His car swerved off the highway, bounced through a bog, and landed in a ditch 435 feet away. Awakened by the crash, Kilmer grasped the steering wheel to keep

Kilmer lugs the ball for UCLA against arch-rival USC during a 1960 clash.

from being thrown out of the car. He was knocked under the dashboard, and the steering wheel bent as he struggled to hang on.

His right leg had been caught under the brake pedal, and his ankle was broken and badly mangled. Water was coming into the car. His chin was badly cut, and there was a deep gash under his right eye. Rescuers had to pry off the doors of the car with crowbars.

The first doctor who examined Kilmer feared his leg would have to be taken off. Two days after the accident, Bill had a four-hour operation on his leg, chin, and eye. He remained in the hospital three months. It looked like the end of a football career for Kilmer. The following June, he had another operation on his leg.

But Kilmer refused to give up football. He missed the 1963 season, played briefly for the 49'ers in 1964, and did not play in 1965. In 1966, he threw only 16 passes. At many games he would silently plead with coach Jack Christiansen to let him get into the game.

Kilmer was sent to New Orleans in the expansion draft early in 1967. He played four years there.

Billy Kilmer and Charley Harraway (far right) combine for a short gain during the 1973 Super Bowl matching the Redskins and the Miami Dolphins.

125

Kilmer, Billy

Then George Allen took over the Washington Redskins in 1971. Kilmer was the first player he went after. Allen had to give up one player and a fourth- and eighth-round draft choice to get Kilmer. "There is something about Kilmer," said Allen. "I don't know if it's charisma, but it is a fierce determination to win and the ability to lead. When he was at New Orleans and I was with the Rams, we played them twice a year. The Saints never should have been in those games. But Billy made them close."

At Washington, Kilmer was Sonny Jurgensen's backup through the five pre-season games of 1971. But he replaced Jurgensen when Sonny injured his shoulder two weeks before the season opened. Kilmer lost the job when Jurgensen recovered, but he was back on the field when Jurgensen went down with an Achilles tendon injury.

"I can win," Kilmer said. And he did. Later he said, "The confidence my team showed in me was as important as the confidence coach Allen had in me."

Kilmer had once been a fine runner, but he had lost that ability in his auto accident. Now he directed the Redskins with spirit and brilliance, and his passes hit their mark.

The following season, in the National Football Conference (NFC) championship game, Kilmer

Kilmer barks out signals for the New Orleans Saints.

was the key man in the defeat of Dallas, 26-3. He completed 14 of 18 passes, including touchdown throws of 16 and 45 yards to wide receiver Charley Taylor. Kilmer also let fly a 51-yard bomb to Taylor to set up Washington's first score. Kilmer had come back from painful injury and years of slow recovery to be one of the league's best.

After defeating Dallas, the Redskins moved into the Super Bowl against the Miami Dolphins but lost, 14-7. In the four seasons following the Redskins' Super Bowl appearance, Kilmer led the team to three more playoff berths.

Time and time again in clutch situations, Kilmer led Washington to victory when a game seemed to be out of reach. At 36, he had one of his finest years as a passer in 1975. He threw a career high of 23 touchdown passes. Billy Kilmer was released by the Redskins following the 1978 season.

Because of his own battles against physical handicaps, Kilmer's determination was always present during his career. "Victory is the only thing," he says. "It brings pride, money, championships. It's the bread and butter of the game."

Twice fighting off injuries that were certain to end his career, Billy Kilmer received the Most Courageous Athlete Award in 1971.

Leading the Redskins to the National Football Conference title in 1972, Kilmer made good use of the short pass.